DIVINE ALIGNMENT

DIVINE ALIGNMENT

SQUIRE RUSHNELL

HOWARD BOOKS
A DIVISION OF SIMON & SCHUSTER, INC.
New York · Nashville · London · Toronto · Sydney · New Delhi

Howard Books
A Division of Simon & Schuster, Inc.
1230 Avenue of the Americas
New York, NY 10020

Scripture quotations marked (NIV) are taken from the HOLY BIBLE,
NEW INTERNATIONAL VERSION®. Copyright © 1973, 1978, 1984
International Bible Society. Used by permission of Zondervan. All rights reserved.

Scripture quotations marked KJV are taken from the King James Version of the Bible.

Scripture quotations marked The Message are taken from The Message. Copyright © 1993, 1994, 1995,
1996, 2000, 2001, 2002. Used by permission of NavPress Publishing Group.

Scripture quotations marked (NASB) are taken from the New American Standard Bible®, Copyright ©
1960, 1962, 1963, 1968, 1971, 1972, 1973, 1975, 1977, 1995 by
The Lockman Foundation. Used by permission. (www.Lockman.org)

Scripture marked (ISV) are taken from The Holy Bible:
International Standard Version is Copyright © 1994–2009 by the ISV Foundation.
ALL RIGHTS RESERVED INTERNATIONALLY. The entire contents of this site are
Copyright © 1996–2009 by the ISV Foundation.
ALL RIGHTS RESERVED INTERNATIONALLY.

First Howard Books hardcover edition July 2012

HOWARD and colophon are trademarks of Simon & Schuster, Inc.

For information about special discounts for bulk purchases, please contact
Simon & Schuster Special Sales at 1-866-506-1949 or business@simonandschuster.com.

The Simon & Schuster Speakers Bureau can bring authors to your live event.
For more information or to book an event, contact the Simon & Schuster Speakers Bureau
at 1-866-248-3049 or visit our website at www.simonspeakers.com.

Designed by Ruth Lee-Mui

Manufactured in the United States of America

1   3   5   7   9   10   8   6   4   2

Library of Congress Cataloging-in-Publication Data
Rushnell, Squire D.
Divine alignment / by Squire Rushnell.
p. cm.
Includes bibliographical references (p.).
1. Prayer—Christianity. 2. Spiritual life—Christianity. 3. Spirituality. 4. Christian life. I. Title.
BV210.3.R865 2012
248.3'2—dc23
2011046411

ISBN 978-1-4516-4856-0
ISBN 978-1-4516-4857-7 (ebook)

To all the ardent readers who have helped propel the term godwinks into the language . . . thank you!

CONTENTS

DIVINE ALIGNMENT

SPEAK WITH
THE NAVIGATOR

L et us begin by understanding Divine Alignment.

The Hertz rent-a-car agent advised that any vehicle could be equipped with a GPS navigational device—called "Never Lost."

I remember thinking: *Wouldn't it be great if we all had GPS; a Global Positioning System . . . making sure we are "never lost"?*

That's when the penny dropped.

We do.

EACH OF US IS BORN WITH A BUILT-IN GPS. GOD'S POSITIONING SYSTEM.

Right from birth, we come equipped with a highly sophisticated navigational package that—through an internal voice of intuition and godwinks—divinely aligns us with people, as well as events, who assist us in reaching our destiny and keep us from losing our way.

Let me expand on that.

When that telephone call that "just happened" to connect you with someone who "coincidentally" placed you on a whole new track, or you bumped into that person who, oh so serendipitously, led you to a life-changing experience—a new job, a relationship, or a geographical move—**you were encountering Divine Alignment, guided by your personal GPS.**

I suspect you never stopped to ask, "*Why* was that person at that precise place, at that exact time, in order for me to bump into them?" Or, "*Why* did that phone call occur at that auspicious moment?"

Does this describe you? Day in and day out you nonchalantly encounter one person after another as you bound from one event to the next, casually accepting life as a series of accidents. Only when you stop to open your mind to the immense possibilities of Divine Alignment do you begin to see the marvelous connections and invisible threads that connect you from one person to another. You begin to understand that your life is not an accident at all. You're not like a twig randomly floating down a stream to destinations unknown.

You begin to see the marvelous connections and invisible threads that connect you from one person to another.

Yet, as you travel through life, *your* hands are on the steering wheel most of the way. And one of the gifts you are given, factory installed, is *free will.*

You're free to go too fast or too slow. To be reckless or responsible. Or even free to drive off the highway altogether, if that's what you choose.

You also have the free will to acknowledge . . . or to ignore . . . that you are not here by accident.

The truth is, you are part of an incredible plan that was programmed into your DNA long before you were born.

How do you access that plan?

Within your own personal GPS you have a Navigator. Someone much bigger than you—and all of us—guiding your life.

The question is, *How* do you tune in? How do you communicate with the Navigator? How do you determine what purpose He has planned uniquely and especially for you?

Very simply—you communicate with Him.

HOW DO YOU COMMUNICATE WITH THE NAVIGATOR?

The best way is simply by talking with Him. The same way you'd talk with your father or grandfather. We have a word for it:

Prayer.

DON'T LET THAT WORD STARTLE YOU

I've searched my mind for a euphemism—another word that isn't so, shall we say, unnerving—conceding that we are living in a society that is hypersensitive to political correctness. These days we've become so gun-shy we bolt from anything that smacks of religion.

In fact, you could be asking, "Should I drop this book here and now? I don't want to read a religious book!"

This one isn't. It's spiritual, hopefully inspiring, but not religious.

Remind yourself that this book is written neither by Einstein nor by Billy Graham. It's written by me, one of the fathers of ABC's *Schoolhouse Rock!* A guy who brought you TV cartoons on Saturday morning. So, how theologically heady can it be?

Okay, regarding that little word we're discussing, to be completely honest, I can't conjure up a different word from the English language—other than *prayer*—to express what I want to say.

Moreover, prayer is not just a word we use in English. It's a concept integral to every faith and probably every language.

So, I hope you're in accord; in the absence of *In the absence of a suitable substitute, the word* prayer *is a perfectly fine choice.*

a suitable substitute, the word *prayer* is a perfectly fine choice. Let us therefore boldly welcome it to our lips along with other expressions, like *talk*, *speak*, or *chat*.

Programming her personal GPS by chatting with the Navigator—through prayer—is exactly what Carla did. Let's let her story exemplify the concept.

CARLA'S CHAT

It seemed perfectly plausible when Carla's friend called, looking for support.

"Alice was trying to have a baby and she wanted me to come to her apartment while she took the home pregnancy test," she remembers.

But when she got to her friend's place, Carla learned that Alice had purchased *two* pregnancy tests—one for herself and another as a control for Carla to administer.

"Sure, why not," replied Carla, glad to help out.

One of the tests indicated a positive result. The other did not.

"But we were confused and surprised," says Carla, "because the positive one was *mine!*"

The two women rushed back to the pharmacy, purchased two more tests, and repeated the procedure. The results were the same.

"I quickly called my ob-gyn," explains Carla, "who took me in for examination that very afternoon. He did an ultrasound, and sure enough, there was the little tyke."

Carla's emotions took off like a roller coaster. The surprise of discovering her pregnancy, at a time when her life was already in turmoil, ushered in all kinds of uncertainties, contrasted with the unexpected joy that she was going to have a baby!

During the next few days she began to worry and doubt if she was worthy of being a mother; she started cramping and bleeding.

Worried, she rushed back to the doctor's office.

The ultrasound was repeated. But, tragically, what was revealed on the screen was a shock; she had lost her baby.

"I was devastated," whispers Carla.

The sadness was so overwhelming that she could hardly comprehend what the doctor was telling her to do—to come back in, in a couple of days, and have a D&C procedure to prevent infection.

Carla returned home. Her cloak of grief drew tight around her. She cried and cried. She remained in bed.

"I can't describe the feeling, except to say that I felt like I was being pushed down . . . I felt heavy."

She stayed home from work, skipped the D&C appointment, took no phone calls, and didn't crawl from bed for a week.

"I was despondent . . . I continued to cry and cry. I thought I might be experiencing some normal depression following a miscarriage."

She didn't know what to do, or to whom she could turn. So . . . she called upon the Navigator.

"I was so completely distraught that I prayed, and prayed, and prayed. I begged God to please let it all be a mistake, that the doctors were wrong, promising to be the best mother in the world if I just had one more chance. I really believed I could get the baby back, somehow, if I prayed hard enough."

When Carla finally pulled herself out of bed, she called the doctor and went to his office.

"He was a little mad at me for not showing up for my appointment," she recalls.

Anticipating that he might scold her, she cautiously told him that she thought she might still be pregnant.

The doctor just looked at her sympathetically. He'd heard this before.

"You're having a normal reaction to the trauma of losing a baby," he said, choosing his words carefully. "Many women feel this way after a miscarriage. But . . ." he continued with firmness, "it's very important now for you to have the D&C."

Carla looked at him directly. She nodded slightly.

"I will. Provided you give me one more ultrasound."

He stared at her a moment. Then, reluctantly, he agreed.

She quietly lay on the examining table as the doctor and nurses prepped for the ultrasound. They ran the instrument over her tummy while looking at the results on the screen.

And there, in black and white, was the very definite shape of a baby!

Carla could not believe her eyes, which were filling with tears of joy and relief as her lower lip began to quiver.

The doctor was speechless.

"I can't explain it," he said.

It remained unsaid, yet everyone in the room thought it: *Thank God Carla was motivated to skip the D&C.* For surely, had she not missed her appointment, there would have been no baby.

To this day Carla remains astonished with the series of events, and how her pleadings to the Navigator resulted in an outcome that no one could have predicted.

Her daughter is now sixteen years old and Carla has lived up to her promise to devote herself to raising her. She left her career behind to be a full-time mother and has no regrets. She thanks God every day for giving her the strength to believe in her own senses, overriding the doctors, when they were so certain that she was wrong and they were right.

Programming her personal GPS by talking with the Navigator . . . prayer . . . worked.

HOW DO YOU PRAY?

Very simply, prayer is communication with someone up there bigger than you. God.

Prayer doesn't require pomp and circumstance.

It needn't be executed on your knees.

You don't have to say "thees" and "thous."

You don't even have to speak out loud. You can talk to God inside your head or write Him a letter.

Let me expand on that thought. I remember the time an elderly country gentleman named Ralph Lankler told me, with a twinkle in his eye, "I write a letter to God every morning."

"Really?"

"Yep."

"What do you say?"

"Oh, I just tell Him whatever's on my mind—thank Him for the gifts He's sent since my last letter."

"How do you sign it?"

"Love, Ralph."

Hmm. Nice idea, isn't it?

My point is this: You just need to *communicate* with your Navigator—God—the way you would with your dad or a loved and respected grandparent. When you do, you'll discover it's your daily dialogue with Him that enables you to effectively program your GPS.

It is during these quiet times with your Maker that you are also giving Him an opportunity to speak to you, through the still small voice within. You may be surprised at the number of times, during prayer, that a perfect idea pops into your head. During these moments of complete attention, you are more apt to be actively listening for God's guidance.

CAN I TALK TO THE NAVIGATOR ABOUT ANYTHING?

Basically, yes.

The Bible provides you with that permission.

If you remain in me and my words remain in you,
ask whatever you wish, and it will be done for you.

JOHN 15:7 (NIV)

WHAT ABOUT SOMETHING REALLY IMPOSSIBLE?

Let me introduce another story that will most likely cause you to say "that's impossible," notwithstanding the empirical evidence that I'm going to lay right in front of you.

TONI AND DAVID

Toni Espinoza, a forty-eight-year-old mother of two, looked into her friend's doubtful eyes.

She had just quietly told him something she knew would be difficult for anyone to understand. But Crawford Higgins was a longtime family friend. Over the years Toni and her husband, David, had shared many family issues with Crawford and his wife. They'd grown up together. Their kids played together. They attended the same church. Toni and David valued Crawford's opinion.

"Toni, are you crazy?" said Crawford bluntly.

They'd just been talking about the issue that had gripped their two families for several weeks, ever since David had been told by three different cardiologists that unless he had a heart transplant, he would die. Perhaps within months.

The two couples had shared information about every doctor's visit. They pooled medical research each had done. They had prayed for David's survival. But now Toni was sharing a secret with Crawford—that she had prayed for something else—confirmation that David would be well, by asking God to make it snow in their Mexican border community of McAllen, Texas. On Christmas Day!

"Toni, you've lived here all your life," Crawford said, incredulously. "Have you ever even seen snow?"

She slowly shook her head and smiled.

Crawford stared back at her.

"Do you know the last time we got snowflakes in McAllen?" He didn't wait for an answer. "A hundred and nine years ago."

Toni smiled again. For inexplicable reasons, she had peace in her heart that surpassed all understanding.

But Crawford wasn't finished.

"And . . . it has *never* snowed on Christmas Day."

Toni and David Espinoza, both in their late forties, live in a modest home on a quiet street of McAllen, which sits on the southernmost border of the United States and Mexico, five and a half hours south of Houston. In the dead of winter "cold," in McAllen it is seventy degrees.

Toni and David were grateful for lives abundant in joy and values. Their marriage was nearly thirty years strong, and Trisha and Lisa, their two daughters, were out of the nest and on their way.

Then the devastating news hit them like a ton of bricks.

It was midyear 2004 and David was advised that congestive heart failure had enlarged and damaged his heart to such an extent that it was working at only 10 percent capacity.

"We're surprised he's still walking," said each doctor they saw, in so many words.

"A heart transplant is your only option," they echoed. "Without it, you've only got months to live."

Soon Toni and David were driving up to Houston for further evaluations at the famed DeBakey Heart Center at Baylor Hospital. There, it was confirmed that David's ejection fraction, which should be in the normal range of 50 to 70 percent, was only 15 to 20 percent.[1]

Ejection fraction (EF) is defined this way: "A test that determines how well your heart pumps with each beat."[2]

DeBakey doctors advised David that it was prudent to put him on the list for a heart donor, warning that it often takes nine months or more to find a perfect match. Even if one were found, the transplant would need to take place within about three hours. Given the distance between McAllen and Houston, that would be another serious issue.

Toni and David clung to each other.

The report of each doctor made them feel pummeled. Yet what could they do but grasp for strands of hope that they would be delivered a miracle and somehow pull through?

Arriving at the most critical crossroads of their lives—with life or death hanging in the balance and the couple consumed by uncertainty—they did what you might have done; they prayed. Without even realizing it, they were programming their personal GPS by speaking to the Navigator. God.

Praying several times a day, Toni cried out to God to save her husband. Yet even as she did this, she became more and more conflicted with the awareness that in order for David to live, someone else had to die.

"That doesn't seem right," she discerned.

So, instead of a transplant, she asked God for a miraculous healing.

By early December both Toni and David were feeling a tentative peace about the ordeal, somewhat like a cease-fire in battle.

"I felt we were in God's hands," said David.

"I believed that God had already begun working to heal my husband," said Toni.

Yet she wanted something more, some kind of tangible assurance that God's miracle was forthcoming.

She spoke with the Navigator about it, privately.

"Lord, I will know David is okay, if you make it snow on Christmas Day, here in McAllen, Texas," she stated flatly.

She mentioned this to David. But when he didn't respond—one of those times that husbands don't really listen, David said later—she decided to drop the matter with him. Instead, she told three others about her pact with God: Crawford Higgins, their close family friend; her sister Sylvia; and her friend Marilyn.

"Snow in McAllen? That's impossible," said her sister.

Crawford was simply blunt. "Toni, if you're expecting it to snow here, where we've lived all our lives, and never seen snow—let alone on Christmas Day—you might as well start planning the funeral."

Toni nodded.

Christmas Eve arrived.

At eleven-thirty Toni looked through the sliding-glass doors into the backyard and blinked. Snow flurries were falling.

"Trisha!" she shouted to her daughter, home for the holidays from New York City. "That's snow, isn't it?" She wasn't sure, having never seen snow.

"Yes!"

They embraced.

"Your dad's going to be okay," whispered Toni, choking back tears. "Quick, go get Dad and Lisa."

David, struggling with a cold and setting an early alarm for his Santa chores, had gone to bed early.

Toni slid open the door to the backyard and stepped onto the lawn, now speckled with snow.

Coatless, alone with God, she lifted her face to the heavens, and closed her eyes as white flecks of snow dotted her hair and stuck to her smiling face.

"Thank You, Lord. Thank You."

The next morning, Christmas Day, bundled-up children of McAllen burst from their homes to manufacture first-time-ever snowmen and fanned angels on front lawns. And, for the first time in recorded history, McAllen, Texas, received a white Christmas. The city's first measurable snow in 109 years.[3] The newspaper heralded the rare event with a special section.

●　　●　　●

Four weeks later Toni and David drove back to Houston for three days of previously scheduled tests at the DeBakey Heart Center. On the third morning Dr. Guillermo Torre entered the small office holding David's chart.

He studied it, checking and rechecking the name on top.

His eyes began to widen. His jaw dropped. He looked up at the two of them.

"I can't explain this," he said with surprise in his voice. "You're not sick anymore!"

He again looked at the chart. Again looked up.

"David, you're going to be around for a long time."

For anyone who doubts that Toni's prayers were answered with remarkable godwinks, following continued conversations with the Navigator, the medical records from the DeBakey Heart Center tell the story.[4] On David's initial visit, April 27, 2004, doctors wrote: "LV function is severely depressed with LVEF [Left Ventricle Ejection Fraction] 15 to 20 percent." Normal, if you recall, is 50 to 70 percent. However, four weeks after the white Christmas miracle in McAllen, on January 24, 2005, the report states: "Lower limits normal LV function. Qualitative EF is 50 percent," within the lower range of normal.

> If you have faith as small as a mustard seed,
> you can say to this mountain, "Move from
> here to there," and it will move.
> Nothing will be impossible for you.
>
> MATTHEW 17:20

BUT WHAT IF *MY* REQUEST TO GOD IS REALLY *REALLY* IMPOSSIBLE?

Measure whatever problems you have, whatever issues you're wrestling with, against this man's. Don was happily driving home one day from a conference and suddenly he was looking at the front end of an eighteen-wheeler truck coming through his windshield. His car was crushed. He was dead in a matter of moments.

Could your problems be any worse than that?

How could Don . . . how could you . . . how could *anyone* get out of Don Piper's predicament?

One word: prayer.

But you just said he was dead!!

Yes, he was in an impossible situation. He was dead. But, for the Navigator, nothing's impossible.

You perhaps read Don Piper's story; his book *Ninety Minutes in Heaven* has been a *New York Times* bestseller.

However, I'd like to share a different perspective on Don's amazing story, from the point of view of the man and woman whom God divinely aligned to "just happen" to come along into Don's life—or in this case— . . . Don's death—at the most auspicious time.

ANITA, DICK, AND DON: MIRACLE ON THE BRIDGE

"I've got to have a cup of real coffee! My headache's getting worse," said Anita, her brows tightening, as she motioned to the upcoming Dairy Queen.

Who could have ever known that Anita's urgent need for a cup of coffee was about to alter her life, forever intertwining it with the lives of others? Looking back, that cup of coffee would become a critical godwink, in her life, and in the lives of others.

Anita and her husband, Dick Onarecker, had spent that cold rainy January morning attending a conference in East Texas where decaf-only coffee was served. Anita had learned the hard way that without "real" coffee in her system, a throbbing headache was just around the corner.

Resuming the two-hour drive home, cradling the cup with both hands, Anita blinked and moved slightly forward as she looked through the windshield. A fog was still hovering over a bridge they were approaching, and something looked odd. It was an accident. There was a big truck, an eighteen-wheeler, stopped in the wrong lane! Two men stood outside the truck, looking around. One wore what looked like an officer's uniform.

Dick slowed down and the tires made crunching sounds as he steered onto the bridge, around the debris littering the road.

They passed a damaged car resting just beyond the truck. In that car, a man, stunned, seemed to be staring blankly as he sat behind the wheel.

They passed an object Anita could barely make out—logic told her it was another car—but it was no longer shaped like a car. It was flattened, crushed, and still steaming. The big truck must have run right over it!

Dick swerved around the flattened vehicle, pulled ahead on the bridge, and stopped. They both jumped out and began walking back. Approaching the flattened car, Anita and Dick could see there was a bloodied body inside.

Acknowledging his wife's sensitivity to blood and gore, Dick spoke quickly. "Why don't you go on over to that other car," he said seriously, nodding in the direction of the other vehicle. "Maybe you can help that person."

She was relieved.

Soon Anita was leaning through a smashed-out window of the first car, speaking softly, calming an older man who was still stunned, seated behind the wheel. She handed him her still-warm cup of coffee.

Shocked by the carnage—a horrible accident that must have occurred only a couple of minutes before—Dick surveyed the flattened wreckage of what was once a Ford Escort. *No one could survive this,* he quickly assessed.

The uniformed man, a prison guard, approached and stood next to him. They nodded at each other. Glancing past him, Dick could see the name of a nearby state prison etched on the cab of the truck.

"Don't bother with him. I already checked," said the guard, motioning at the wreckage with his head. "He's dead."

Dick stepped past the man, past a piece of human bone in the road, and bent down to peer into the mangled pile of metal. There was the body of a man, twisted and lifeless. To satisfy himself, he reached in, felt for a pulse; there was none.

What should he do? What could he do?

Pray for the man, was a clear, decisive command from within his mind. An urgent, voiceless message to pray for a dead man, to pray that he would live, and that he would have no internal injuries.

That makes no sense! he silently argued. *The man is dead. Why pray for a dead man?*

Dick was a pastor. He'd learned obedience. He knew the principles of talking with the Navigator. And that "All things were possible." Still, he hesitated to pray.

A police officer approached the wreckage; he too attempted to locate a pulse.

"We have one fatality here," said the policeman into his two-way radio.[5]

Dick again felt the compulsion to pray. *Have I gone nuts?* he thought, resisting the urge that wouldn't leave his mind.

An emergency medical technician was the next official to verify that the man was dead.

Finally, surrendering to, and even oddly emboldened by, God's insistent directive, Dick began to pray—out loud—loud enough for others to hear, as ridiculous as it seemed, for a period of time he could not determine. He kept his hand firmly on the dead man's right shoulder, beseeching that he would come back to life, with no internal injuries.

•   •   •

The dead man was Don Piper.

Had he been able to speak at that moment, he would have said, "The last thing I remember was driving onto the bridge and suddenly everything became dark.[6] Then I remember being at the gates of heaven, surrounded by people, and hearing music."

Don Piper's spirit had been transported to heaven while his body remained entrapped in the wreckage of an accordioned Ford Escort.

The tractor-trailer truck had crossed into his lane and rolled over his car, crushing every part of his body except his right arm. He had died instantly.[7] And instantly he went to heaven—for the next hour and a half.

Anita watched as EMTs tended to the man she'd been watching over, then walked back to her own car to sit and wait for Dick. She observed the activity of emergency workers and vehicles. And waited. Again and again she looked at her watch. Dick was away a long time.

Respecting God's command, in total defiance of human logic, Dick prayed boldly.

"I prayed aloud, nonstop," said Dick.

Dick continued his prayer for the survival of a dead man. He prayed and prayed. And when he became exhausted verbally, he prayed musically; he sang a favorite old hymn.

"What a friend we have in Jesus . . ."

He heard something. A weak voice.

It was the dead man! He was singing along with him!

Dick spoke to him. The man spoke back. Dick then rushed to the ambulance driver.

"Come get this man. Take him to the hospital. He needs immediate care!"

"The driver looked at me as if I were out of my mind," says Dick. "But I gave him no leeway."

The disbelieving EMT walked to the wrecked car, moved close enough to hear the man's subdued voice, then sprang into action.

Don Piper had been dead for an estimated ninety minutes. He went to heaven and came back to earth. Today he lives and believes he has a mission to tell about it, to describe scenes that no one could imagine.

"Everybody I saw there had hair," says Don Piper, reassuring his attentive audiences. "In heaven you'll be perfect in every way, just the way God made you before age and circumstances of life have stolen anything from you. You'll be perfect.

"For example, my grandmother had false teeth," he continues, "but when I saw her in heaven her teeth were real. Her body was perfect."[8]

"My grandfather . . . reached out to me with hands that were no longer missing fingers, as on earth . . . saying, 'Welcome home, Donny.'"[9]

It took Don Piper two years before he could tell anyone about his experiences in the realm known as heaven. Partly, he says, because he didn't think earthly words could describe what he saw. But also because he didn't think anyone would believe him.

Subsequently Don overcame each of these concerns with his national bestselling book *Ninety Minutes in Heaven*. His vivid promises of what we can expect have been a source of encouragement to many.

"The music was my most precious memory of heaven. I carry it with me to this day . . . the singing of thousands of songs at the same time. There was no chaos. I could distinguish each one of them with my heavenly ear."[10]

"Heaven is kind of a sensory explosion . . . sights, sounds, touch, aromas, everything was just magnificent."[11]

He describes it as a great reunion. "The people who greet you at the gates of heaven will be those who've gone before you . . . who helped you get there." He cites Miss Norris, a lady who used to take him to church as a child and introduced him to Jesus. "She greeted me at the gate of heaven."[12]

Don describes the beauty: the gate has a pearliness, and leads to a street of gold. "The lights reflecting off the gate made it look like it's pulsating with life. That's because in heaven there is no artificial light—God illuminates with His glory."

Everything he saw was magnificent. It gave him a wonderful feeling.

"It's awesome. It's incredible. I heard incredible sounds . . . the sound of angel's wings hovering all about me—not all angels have wings, but many of them do—I felt wonderful, never happier in my life."

As with others who have said they experienced heaven, Don did not wish to return to earth.

"I was focused on seeing the Lord. Then, suddenly, everything began to go dark again. The aroma began to fade. The sounds began to fade. I was about to ask, 'What's going on?' but before I could say anything, everything went dark. Stopped. It was pitch dark. And I heard a voice . . . a voice I'd never heard before. It was singing, 'What a friend we have in Jesus.'"

Dick Onarecker stood dumbfounded, watching the ambulance carrying Don pull away from the bridge as the second stanza of the old hymn resonated in his mind: "What a privilege to carry, everything to God in prayer." It seemed like such an understatement.

"Eventually Dick returned to our car, and sat next to me," says Anita. But before he could relay, in detail, the incredible events that had happened, he needed to make an urgent phone call.

"At the top of the first hill was a small store with a pay phone. I waited again as he phoned the man's church in Alvin."

Returning to the car Dick told Anita what happened on the bridge—how at least four different persons, including himself, had declared the man dead.

"I tried to find the man's pulse, but there wasn't any."[13]

He told Anita how he he'd been compelled to pray for the dead man. That he prayed and prayed and sang a hymn . . . and how shocked he was when the man spoke and sang along with him.

"I asked him, 'Friend, are you a Christian?' He said yes, told me his name, about his church in Alvin, and his wife, Eva."

Several days later Dick and Anita visited Don at a hospital in Houston.

"I enjoyed meeting Eva, Don's lovely wife," said Dick. "She described the many injuries to Don's arms and legs, all over his body. Then she commented with a questioning tone, 'Our doctors are baffled because, with all that happened to him, they can't find any internal injuries.'"

There was a momentary pause. Dick looked at Anita, then turned and smiled at Eva.

"I have it on good authority," said Dick. "Your husband will live!"

"I survived because of prayer," says Don Piper. "One man, Dick Onarecker, felt God impress upon him to pray and he did. He prayed me back to this earth."[14]

Dick always wondered how many lives would have turned out differently if his dear wife, Anita, had not been profoundly affected by decaffeinated coffee, if she hadn't had the headache, if, that morning, she hadn't said, "Will you stop at that Dairy Queen so I can get a cup of coffee?"[15]

Anita had another haunting thought. *If we had not stopped to get my coffee, Richard and I would have been in the car that was run over.*

A godwink.

She has written her and Dick's compelling story in a book called *Divine Appointment.*

Later on in this book, we'll revisit the Don Piper story, comparing the details of his experience with several others who say they physically left this earth and went to a place called heaven. The parallels in these stories are extraordinary.

But, the message of this chapter again, is this: regardless of how impossible your situation is—whether you're facing a mountain of stress and worry so immense you're having difficulty sleeping—or whether you've lost a job, not knowing where, or how, to start over, and insurmountable financial problems have pitted you against giant unfair institutions and the government—perhaps your problems *still* are not as bad as Don Piper's. And maybe not as bad as David Espinoza's death sentence. Yet, the way for you to scale that mountain, or pull yourself out of the hole you're in, is to program your GPS the same way they did: Talk to the Navigator. And listen.

CAN MERE WORDS MAKE A DIFFERENCE?

Can mere words uttered to an unseen Navigator really make a difference?

Yes.

Words you speak internally or externally to an unseen God *will* make an *unbelievable difference* in your life.

I know, it's hard to get your mind around a concept like that if you've been convinced otherwise all your life.

But think about this: there are many things in your life that you accept based upon *outcome*, not because you know *how it works*.

Imagine standing in your kitchen eighty-five years ago; someone tells you that a box would soon be available, into which you could place a cup of water, and by pressing a few buttons, *invisible rays* would make it hot in sixty seconds. *How* does a microwave work? Beats me, but it works. I trust it . . . based on *outcome*.

Another person, decades ago, says something even more far-fetched. Soon there'd be a way that the image and voice of a person speaking in Hong Kong could travel invisibly through the air to be seen, at the flick of a switch, on a box in your living room.

Absurd? Invisible rays heating water? Someone transported invisibly through the air from around the world?

Truth is, most of us have no idea how microwaves or television sets work. We just know that when we follow certain steps, they produce an outcome that we accept.

That's how prayer works in your life. Taking steps, talking with the Navigator, and focusing on outcome—not on *how it works*.

Let me share a story that brings this premise back to everyday life—a situation you can relate to; a regular gathering of teachers to discuss concerns about students, and to pray for them. Yes, despite all the misinterpretation about "separation of church and state" these days, it is perfectly legal for teachers to speak with the Navigator on behalf of their students.

AN ALLISON MOMENT

Randy Reed, teacher and coach, made it a point to carve out a little time with several of his fellow teachers, once a week, before the start of classes, to share mutual concerns.

"I started by telling them about a book I'd recently read, *When God Winks*, which talked about how so-called coincidences in our lives are more than random happenings," recalls Randy. "After the book discussion, we began to offer prayer requests as we usually do."

One of the teachers brought up a sweet girl named Allison, a former student who had moved to another school district.

"Our real concern was that the school Allison was now attending had a really rough reputation," says Randy. "We wondered how she was coping, and began discussing how we could check on her."

At that moment, over the intercom, came an announcement that there was a phone call for Randy.

"Thinking it was probably a parent letting me know their son would not be at practice that afternoon, or something to that effect, I told the other teachers that I'd ignore the announcement and return to it later," says Randy.

They continued their discussion about Allison.

"I then had a strong feeling that I should answer the call," says Randy, excusing himself from the meeting.

In the front office he picked up the phone.

"Coach Reed here."

"Hi, Coach, it's Allison."

There was a moment of silence.

"Coach Reed, are you there?"

"Yes, Allison, I'm here. I just can't believe it's you . . . We were just talking about you. Are you okay?"

"I was getting ready for school," she explained, "and had a feeling I should call you and let you know that I am doing fine. My new school is different, but I like it okay."

They spoke for a few minutes, then Randy rejoined his meeting, reporting the extraordinary godwink to the others.

Today he recalls how stunned he was. "I'd never received a call at the school from a student. And, to get this call, at this time, was incredible. It was a beautiful example of God answering a prayer, and in this case, even before our prayers were completed."

• • •

When you program your GPS regularly, through conversations with the Navigator, you too will experience answered prayers—or, another term for that: godwinks.

Let me share one more illustration to make the point of this chapter.

NATHAN'S STORY

Nathan Christensen was a good kid. An athlete. Growing up in a small Wisconsin farm community. Not the type who would needlessly create worry for his parents, even when driving alone in his mother's Chevy convertible six months after getting his sixteen-year-old driver's license. Nor was he the type to drive without a seat belt.

County Highway X was a stretch of rarely traveled country road running alongside a wildlife preserve in western Wisconsin, a shortcut between Marshfield and Necedah. Not much on it. Almost no houses and lots of deer. That's what it was known for and why so few people took it. The deer were a nuisance, coming off the preserve to lick road salt, jumping in front of cars unexpectedly.

It was a clear, cold night in April, past ten. There were no lights. No cars. No people. Just Nathan and the night.

What did it feel like to go the speed limit, fifty-five miles per hour? For a boy with exceptional prowess in tucking a football under an arm, harmlessly plowing past multiple opponents, it was a momentary boost of adrenaline. The car sped. A fleeting blur crossed the windshield. A screech of brakes. Then the night became soundless. The car became weightless. The road felt like it was no longer beneath him. It wasn't. He was flying. Over a ditch, over a fence, rolling and crashing, upside down, in a cacophonous crushing of metal!

If he had a memory of it, Nathan might have reconstructed those moments. The deer. The brakes. A flash-thought like, *Uh-oh, I'm in trouble*. But he didn't. His memory was gone.

•   •   •

Kevin Lindow was attending a monthly meeting in Madison. His mom went along with him to keep him company on the long, three-hour drive back to his sheep farm near Marshfield.

"How you gonna go?" asked Mrs. Lindow.

"I'll take 39," said Kevin, acknowledging that a main road, slightly out of the way, was the more prudent option at this time of night. It would be past midnight by the time they got home, and the most direct route, County Highway X, was out of the question. The deer.

Kevin surprised himself when he acted to the contrary. At the spot where the road to 39 intersected with County Highway X, he slowed and turned his pickup truck onto the desolate country road for the final forty-five-minute drive.

"Why are you going this way?" Mrs. Lindow asked.

"I don't know. Something's bothering me, I need to go this way," said Kevin, puzzled with why he would challenge conventional wisdom.

Except for the reflection from snow patches picked up in his headlights, they traveled in pitch dark.

Then he saw something! He slowed to a stop.

"Mom. There was a car upside down!"

Kevin backed up, got out of his truck, and in the headlights saw a young man, shirtless and shoeless, sitting on top of a wrecked car.

His first-responder training at the Chili Volunteer Fire Department kicked in.

The boy was incoherent, like someone awakened from a deep sleep. He was cold to the touch, not shaking, which meant that he was suffering from hypothermia. *To be expected*, thought Kevin, considering the below-freezing temperature.

He reached into the wreckage to locate and touch the catalytic converter, which, he recalled from his training, is the last thing on a vehicle to cool off. It was cold. That meant that the boy could have been there for two hours or so. It was now 12:30 a.m.

"Mom, call 911," shouted Kevin as he pulled two heavy blankets from the truck.

Carefully, he wrapped one blanket around Nathan's neck like a horse collar to stabilize it. He then picked him up, carrying him to the side of the road. Training instructions replayed in his mind: *Minimize movement. Don't attempt to place the victim in another vehicle.* Instead Kevin wrapped his arms around the young man and directed his mother to cover the two of them with the second blanket. She then placed her body against theirs, and the threesome waited. And waited.

It was the better part of an hour before the ambulance arrived, and nearly 2 a.m. when it departed. The boy was placed on a gurney, covered in blankets, attached to a ventilator to keep him breathing, and taken to Marshfield's St. Joseph Hospital thirty to forty minutes away.

Before the ambulance doors closed, Kevin noticed the boy was starting to shiver; that was a good sign. It meant that the body heat generated by Kevin and his mother might have lifted the young man from hypothermia.

As they continued their own journey home, Kevin and his mom chatted, reconstructing their experience; wondering why, against human reasoning, they had taken that untraveled road.

From bits of words mumbled by the boy while wrapped in Kevin's arms, Kevin knew that his name was Nathan Christensen, that he'd visited a girl in Marshfield, and that his car had hit a deer.

Nathan's father, Jim, reached for the phone. It was his wife Carol's voice, but it didn't sound like her; she was hysterical. He couldn't understand what she was saying. Her words were disrupted by wails of sobbing and fear. It was about Nathan. He was in a terrible accident.

Dashing for his car, Jim quickly calculated that he was an hour and a quarter away. He'd been staying with friends while working a construction project.

Equidistant from the hospital in Marshfield, Jim and Carol arrived within minutes of each other.

"Your son is in a coma. He has a one-in-one-hundred chance of surviving," said the doctor solemnly.

One percent! repeated Jim in his mind.

"If he does survive, his injuries are likely to leave him paraplegic, perhaps quadriplegic," the doctor continued.

The way Nathan's injuries were described—a teardrop fracture to the C4 vertebra—meant that an errant piece of chipped bone was in danger of encountering his spinal cord, causing an injury similar to that suffered by actor Christopher Reeve.

As a part-time preacher—supplemented by construction work during the week—Jim knew the power of prayer. He'd studied about it for his degree. Over the years he'd gathered plenty of examples of how prayer has a very clear cause and effect. But now, looking down at his boy, braced, bloodied, and bandaged, lying in a coma with slim prospects for life—this was Jim's new reality: the ultimate test for a pastor—to prove, beyond a shadow of doubt, that prayer works.

But . . . would it? Would his earnest pleadings to the Navigator be heard and honored, thereby rescuing his child from death? Doubting God for a single second was not an option. Jim needed to pray like he'd never prayed before.

Jim hovered at Nathan's side, speaking both to God and to the boy in a soft voice, representing himself as well as Carol, for she was having such difficulty seeing her son in such a state.

For two and a half days Nathan lay in a coma. Jim's mind went to the story of Christ encountering two women, Martha and Mary, who were crying. They said that their brother Lazarus had died.

Jim lifted his Bible and flipped the pages to the book of John. Out loud, over Nathan, he began to read.

"Told that his friend Lazarus had been dead for four days, buried in a cave . . . Jesus wept . . . he went there, looked up to heaven and said, 'Father, thank you for hearing me' . . . then he shouted, 'Lazarus come out!' And the dead man came out . . . his face wrapped in a head cloth.'"

Jim looked down at his son, his head wrapped in bandages. With firmness and urgency, he said, "Nathan, you need to be like Lazarus! To wake up. Tomorrow, you need to wake up, Nathan!"

Over and over Jim repeated his plea to the Navigator. He beseeched God not only to save his son, "But to heal him so there will be no evidence of injury."

Twelve hours later, in his coma, Nathan experienced what he later called "a vision," and with it came a feeling that swept over his body and stayed with him.

"It was overwhelming—there was an unusually bright light— and God leaned down to hug me and placed His head against my shoulder—I couldn't see His face, but I knew it was God. It was the closest feeling to having a parent hug you; or when you've just had a load lifted from your shoulders. It was a warm feeling that lasted two days."

Nathan's eyes began to flutter open . . . he saw glimpses of people.

His lips moved, and he tried to speak.

His father was at his side.

"Dad."

"Who am I?" asked Jim.

"James R. Christensen."

"What's your mother's name?"

"Carol L. Christensen."

"Where are you?"

"In a hospital."

A short while later Nathan said, "Dad. You read to me about Lazarus. You told me to wake up."

Jim had heard about people who could hear words spoken while in a coma, but had never experienced it.

He began putting together the pieces of information.

Emergency workers had concluded that Nathan had been cata-pulted through the windshield of the car. *That* had saved his life, for otherwise he most certainly would have been crushed to death.

Yet, witnesses who examined the wreckage said Nathan was mysteriously thrown from the car even though his seat belt was still snapped closed. "How could he have been lifted up and out of his seat belt?" Jim asked one emergency worker after another. No one had an answer.

Moreover, what extraordinary forces had caused Kevin Lindow to change his mind and take the lonely, danger-filled route home that he and his mother had previously determined was not prudent to travel? Making it more remarkable, Kevin had told Jim that no other vehicle had come down that road in the hour and a half that he and his mother were waiting for the ambulance. What an astonishing gift of Divine Alignment, nudging Kevin to change his mind and take that desolate road.

Jim shook his head to dismiss the horrible thought: What if Kevin had not seen Nathan sitting on top of the wreckage? Or, what if it had been someone else—someone who didn't have Kevin's training to know exactly what to do in an emergency?

As the godwinks and evidence of Divine Alignment began to have greater clarity, Jim was shocked when, a day and a half after Nathan came out of the coma, doctors said that he could go home, wearing a collar brace and leg cast.

Yet, keeping Nathan and his parents focused on the seriousness of his injuries, Dr. Tom Faciszewski, a spinal-cord specialist, looked at Jim somberly and said, "Your son will never return to contact sports."[16] The doctor went on to outline the tasks ahead: Nathan would wear a neck brace for fourteen weeks, and would have to minimize his movements so as not to disturb the teardrop fracture. Subsequent to that, an operation would fuse the broken fragment back where it broke off. At the midpoint of his required time in a neck brace, seven weeks, Nathan would come in for a checkup.

• • •

Six weeks later Nathan, still tiring easily, went to bed early. Since leaving the hospital, he'd adapted to sleeping on his back, his only option with the neck brace.

Nathan said his prayers. "I always prayed for the Lord's healing of myself mentally, physically, and spiritually. I definitely prayed for a miraculous healing," says Nathan.

He closed his eyes, lay still, waiting for sleep to come over him.

His neck suddenly "popped."

"It was three loud popping sounds . . . like hearing knuckles cracking," he recalls. "I was frightened. I didn't dare move. So instead of calling out to anyone, I just lay there until I fell asleep."

A few days later Nathan appeared at Dr. Faciszewski's office for his scheduled seven-week appointment. The doctor's radiologist positioned Nathan in front of an X-ray screen.

After the first X-ray she said, "*Where* is your injury?"

"C4. On the left side."

She motioned for him to reposition himself for a repeat of the X-ray.

"*Where* is it?" she reiterated with withering patience.

"C4. Left side."

"How long ago?"

Looking confused, she again motioned him to the X-ray.

This time she thrust the X-ray at him, in a perturbed fashion, and snapped, "Take this to the doctor." Nathan wondered what he'd done wrong.

Nathan and his mom watched Dr. Faciszewski place the X-ray onto the light box.

"*Where* do you have the injury?" he asked, almost gingerly.

Nathan was about to reply but noticed that *this* X-ray appeared to be different from an earlier one he'd seen.

"C4. Left side. Where's *my* X-ray?" he asked.

"This *is* your X-ray," said the doctor in measured tones, turning slowly to look directly at Nathan.

Puzzled himself, Nathan studied the doctor's face.

"He looked like he'd seen a ghost," said Nathan later.

"It must have been God," Dr. Faciszewski quietly said.

The doctor stared at the X-ray a moment longer and added, "There is no evidence of injury."

These were the same words used by Nathan's father in his fervent prayer at the hospital: "*God please save my son and heal him with no evidence of injury.*"

"Can I take this off?" asked Nathan, touching the neck brace, almost child-like, knowing he'd worn it only half of the intended fourteen week period.

The doctor shrugged slightly, "Well . . . you have no evidence of injury."

Starting to leave the office, Nathan turned; he thought he'd press his luck: "Any . . . restrictions . . . on playing sports?"

The doctor, still attempting to process what he'd witnessed, paused, slowly shook his head, and quietly repeated, "You have no evidence of injury."

A few weeks later the fall semester at school resumed. However the principal and athletic director, still cautious, advised the football coach not to let Nathan play. Notwithstanding this, halfway through the season the coach allowed Nathan to start on the kickoff special team. The boy had two solo tackles in his first game.

Subsequently, the principal and coaches were astonished to witness Nathan's prowess in junior-year wrestling—he led the team in wins and number of pins.

The following year it was determined that Nathan, now a senior, would be able to fully resume football. He played fullback.

Nathan's record as a fullback was nothing short of astonishing:

- Most points scored for a season.
- Most yards gained in a game, 212.
- Most yards averaged per carry, 7.5.
- Most total yards gained for a season, 1150.
- Average touchdowns, 1.5 per game, a school record.

What were the outcomes of this remarkable story?

Nathan is studying to be a youth pastor.

Jim and Carol say that the terrible experience galvanized their marriage.

"Carol and I always got along well," says Jim, reiterating that they were high school sweethearts. "But going through that tragedy brought us closer together and elevated our faith. We pray together more now."

Kevin Lindow, the unexpected hero, says, "This experience strengthened my faith."

He warmly remembers how Jim had greeted him when he'd stopped by the hospital to visit Nathan. "Without you, my son wouldn't be here," Jim said, with tears forming in his eyes.

Why does Kevin think he made the decision to take that road that night? "There is no doubt in my mind: God had a hand in it." Then he adds thoughtfully, "I pray that if one of my children is ever in that situation, someone will stop and help them."

There is a song that expresses Nathan's feelings:

ALIVE

I feel so alive

For the very first time

I can't deny you

I feel so alive

I feel so alive
For the very first time
And I think I can fly

—P.O.D.[17]

THE COMMON DENOMINATOR

What factors are common to each of the foregoing stories?

- Someone was in, or thought to be in, desperate straits.
- Someone—a family member, teachers, or a complete stranger—cried out to the Navigator to intervene, in some cases, to replace death for life.
- Sometimes this person or persons requested that health be restored in a specific manner.
- And, with the exception of Nathan's postcoma prayers, none of the persons communicating with the Navigator was the victim himself.

How could these things have happened? Might they have been just some bizarre series of accidental events? Can't these same kinds of outcomes be realized in your own life . . . pulling you from a desperate situation or saving your own child or family member?

FIVE FREQUENTLY ASKED QUESTIONS

The following five FAQs may address matters still rolling through your mind.

FAQ 1: *What About When You Talk to the Navigator and Nothing Happens?*

More to the point, what happens if you pray and you don't get a miraculous outcome like Don Piper or Nathan Christensen?

When you pray, and think nothing is happening—or worse, that you are being ignored from above—God is still working on your behalf, in ways you cannot see. My wonderful wife, Louise, has compared this idea to a rosebush in winter.

Picture that. A rosebush in the winter looks dead. No signs of life. But beneath the surface of the earth, in the root system, God is causing life to carry on. You know that to be fact only because you've seen the evidence—every winter the rosebush looks dead. Every spring it comes "back to life."

In your life it may appear on the surface that nothing is happening, but in fact, God is working behind the scenes, connecting invisible threads, getting people and events in place for godwinks and Divine Alignments to unfold so your prayers can be answered. Yes, it sometimes takes a long time. Longer than we want. But if you were to research the matter completely, you would find *overwhelming* evidence in both contemporary and ancient history, as recorded in the scriptures, that God *does* answer prayers, even if it takes years.

Sometimes your prayers are answered right away. So quickly it astonishes you.

I love the story I shared in one of my books about the widow who had nowhere to turn. She was at the end of her finances; there was no money to pay the mortgage or utility bills, and she had absolutely no idea where she could get it. With no other option, she took the Bible from the shelf, laid it on the floor, and stood on it. Literally.

"I'm standing on the Word, Father, asking for Your help, just like You asked," she beseeched.

Then, going on her errands for the day, she was astounded when two checks with unexpected income turned up in her post office box. Stopping by the bank to deposit them, she discovered an accounting mistake. The result was exactly the amount she needed—and had prayed for—to cover the mortgage and utility bills.

FAQ 2: *How Do I Know I'm on Track and Programming My GPS Correctly?*

The more you program your GPS, the better you get at it.

Do you recall when you initially used the GPS in your car? You weren't that good at it. Or the first time you used a BlackBerry phone, or tried to set the time on your microwave? The more you input information, the more proficient you became.

Similarly, by communicating with God every day, even multiple times a day, you will soon find that your life is becoming more and more enriched.

And, when you get off track in life, tune in to God's Positioning System. By listening and asking for the Navigator's guidance, you'll reestablish your direction. Similar to those times when you are driving your car down the highway and realize you are "off track," your auto GPS will advise that it is "recalculating." It may instruct you to turn around and go back a few exits.

Your answer from above may come in the form of a new thought that "pops" into your head. Or a divine suggestion from someone you're with. Bottom line: the more you communicate with God, through prayer, the more you and He will be in harmony, which, in turn, allows Him to divinely design your pathways and keep you on track.

FAQ 3: *Can I Actually Hear God's Voice, Like My Navigational Device?*

It is very rare that someone reports they have actually *heard* a human voice they believe to be God.

I, personally, have never heard God speak in an audible voice.

I have, however, communicated with two or three people who firmly believe they have.

Many people who use the phrase "I *heard* God's voice" mean that they *sensed* a clear, authoritative voice spoken *within* them—powerful and different from anything they had ever heard before.

If you're doubting that this could happen, think about the times you've heard a song in your head. It was pretty clear, wasn't it? Right now, can't you silently sing "Silent Night" in your head? Can't you "hear" the song inside your mind?

The vast majority of communications that people say they've received from the Navigator are in the form of an inner, instinctive sense, as discussed in the next chapter, or through the little godwinks that pop up in our lives.

FAQ 4: The Most Frequently Asked Question: How Do I Pray?

As my wife, Louise, and I travel the country, performing and speaking at various venues, including churches, on the extraordinary merits of couples praying together, we find *the* most frequently asked question is "How do you do it?"

Admittedly, at first, the question jarred us.

Then, as time wore on, we became more appreciative of the bewilderment people feel, particularly if they were never *taught* how to pray as adults. Or, in the context of this book, how to program their GPS.

Perhaps, like me, you were *taught* how to pray as a child only by learning the centuries-old ditty that begins, "Now I lay me down to sleep, I pray the Lord my soul to keep." Of course the next line may have scared you silly and kept you awake all night. "If I should die before I wake"—*what?*—"I pray the Lord my soul to take." *Oh, no!*

Seriously, though, other than when you were a child, did anyone ever *teach* you how to pray?

You may have been schooled to memorize the Lord's Prayer, in which case you learned the way Jesus, in the Bible, counseled his disciples on how to pray. But memorizing words, even reciting them at church every Sunday morning, does not *teach* you how to communicate with God on a regular basis.

If you were to recite the same greeting to your mom on the

phone, over and over, I doubt that she'd consider that appropriate communication. Conversely, warm, frequent chats with her, expressing gratitude for all she's done, seeking her wise counsel on issues that are of concern to you, would most likely foster the most robust relationship.

Louise and I often answer the question "How do you pray?" by suggesting that it ought to be like sitting down for a cup of coffee and a bagel with your mom or dad. That easy.

FAQ 5: *How Do I Learn to* Listen *to My Navigator?*

A. PROVIDE FULL ATTENTION.
Giving someone your full attention is the first step to listening.

When you give a professor undivided attention, you'll get more out of the course he's teaching. When you look your boss in the eye and focus, you'll understand what your boss wants from you. When you sit down with your spouse on a regular basis and talk through issues that face every marriage, genuinely attempting to understand what he or she is feeling, you are taking giant steps in creating a happy marriage.

If you genuinely wish to listen to the voice of the Almighty on your GPS, you need to start by giving Him your full attention.

B. ENGAGE GOD IN DAILY COMMUNICATION.
When you engage your GPS Navigator through prayer—out loud or inside your head—every single day, you place yourself in a position for God to speak to you through His unique ways. He sometimes acknowledges you by causing godwinks to happen—the seemingly coincidental experiences that are so astonishing they could only have come from Him.

When you write to God, in a letter or a journal, you increase the likelihood of hearing a directive or thought from God resonating within your mind *while* you are in the act of writing. Most likely you will encounter an inner sense, with such clarity, that you *know* it's a communication directly from above.

C. READ THE INSTRUCTION MANUAL.

This is a document written by many different scribes in order to pre-serve God's philosophy and wishes for mankind. And despite scores of centuries separating the writers, most of whom believed they were taking dictation from the Almighty, there is remarkable consistency and continuity in their communications to us.

It is a document that has been tested and challenged for more than three thousand years, yet it still stands as a brilliant instruction manual for you and me. Extraordinary wisdom is available to each of us by simply reading it.

Where can you find it? In the top drawer of almost every hotel room in America.

The Bible.

Most people who read the Bible on a regular basis soon find that "ideas" or "solutions" come into their minds *while* they are reading.

IN THE FINAL ANALYSIS: WHEN YOU ENGAGE THE NAVIGATOR . . . HE ENGAGES YOU.

This is a promise that each of us has been given, written in the an-cient scriptures:

> Believe you will receive
> everything you ask for in prayer.
>
> MATTHEW 21:22 (NIV)

GPS STEP 1

SPEAK WITH THE NAVIGATOR

Program your GPS. Engage in out-loud or silent communication multiple times a day.

Pray.

LISTEN TO
YOUR INNER COMPASS

How many times have you nearly stepped off a curb, not realizing that an unsuspecting car or truck was about to go whooshing past, barely missing you?

Somehow, you received an alert from an inner warning system—an alarm—which caused you to step back, in just the nick of time.

That inner warning system was instinct.

Instinct can be found in all of the lower kingdoms of nature but is often overridden or masked by the reasoning of us humans. For instance, during the tsunami which took thousands of lives in the Far East, most animals survived; birds, domestic animals and elephants instinctively received warning messages from their inner compasses causing them to move safely inland, while humans, with a superior faculty for reasoning, were caught unawares.

The ancient scriptures foretold that God would speak to us in a "small still voice,"[1] and we receive instinctive, intuitive messages all the time. But we often disregard them like an alarm clock that annoyingly reminds us it's time to get up.

Dismissing our inner compass is usually not in our best interests. We may miss protective communications about right and wrong.

Think about it. Was there ever a wrong, illegal, or sinful thing you did in your life that you didn't, in the deepest fibers of your being, just know was inappropriate for you to be engaging in?

Conversely, your inner directional finder will usually point you in the proper direction.

Let me tell you a story about a man named Francis Collins who discovered that an inner compass is a moral barometer that we are born with. And the acceptance of that fact became a life-changing moment for him.

HOW FRANCIS SAW THE LIGHT

Sometimes we have to open our minds to evaluate an idea that appears audacious, and completely contrary to things your friends are telling you, the way Francis Collins did.

Before I tell you the story, however, let me explain who Dr. Collins is today.

As of this writing, he is the sixteenth director of the National Institutes of Health. The first time I saw Dr. Collins on the news, he was standing between the president of the United States and the prime minister of England, being introduced at the White House as the leader of the Human Genome Project that was mapping the DNA of the human body. This code of human cells in the body was so extensive that if it were to be read out loud, at the rate of three letters per second, it would take thirty-one years to articulate. (Try saying "ABC" in one second; then imagine continuing it for three decades.)

President Clinton told us that Dr. Francis Collins, a rigorously trained scientist, was leading the team "learning the language in which God created life."[2]

A scientist? Coexisting with God? I wondered.

Dr. Collins then spoke. "It is humbling to me," he said, "and awe inspiring, to realize we have caught the first glimpse of our own instruction book, known previously only to God."

My eyebrows lifted as I stared at the TV.

Dr. Francis Collins, most will agree, is a distinguished, intelligent man of science. Yet his beliefs that God and science are compatible are held by only about 40 percent of the scientific community, in his view.[3] During an earlier period in his life, Collins's beliefs about the origin of man were in lockstep with the other 60 percent of scientists: he was an atheist, unable to entertain the thought that human beings could benefit by speaking to an unseen God.

It all changed when a grandmother from North Carolina asked him, "What do you believe?"

Until that time, says Dr. Collins, "I found myself, with a combination of willful blindness and . . . arrogance, having avoided any serious consideration that God might be a real possibility."[4]

But the question the grandmother had asked haunted him. *Does a scientist draw conclusions without considering the data?* he thought.

He thus decided that he should approach the question "Is there a God?" without bias, as a scientist. "Although at first, I was confident that a full investigation of the rational basis for faith would deny the merits of belief, and reaffirm my atheism," he confides.

Dr. Collins studied many books, including one called *Mere Christianity* by former atheist C. S. Lewis. Avenues of thought about "Moral Law," never before traversed, suddenly turned his thinking upside down. He found himself concurring with Lewis's premise, simplified here, that man's ability to discern right from wrong affirms that there must be a God.

"The concept of right and wrong appears to be universal among all members of the human species,"[5] concluded Collins. Moreover, "the force we feel from the Moral Law [is] the altruistic impulse, the voice of conscience calling us to help others even if nothing is received in return."[6]

Dr. Collins was astonished with these conclusions: "This Moral Law shone its bright white light into the recesses of my childish atheism, and demanded a serious consideration of its origin,"[7] he said. "Faith in God now seemed more rational than disbelief."[8]

He discovered that U.S. space scientist Wernher von Braun held similar views. "The knowledge that man can choose between good and evil should draw him closer to his creator,"[9] said von Braun, who had also become a believer.

Francis Collins was forever changed. He deduced that there *is* someone up there listening to us, a benevolent Creator who cares about each of us, and who genuinely hopes we will use the free will He's given us to communicate with Him regularly. By opening his mind, Dr. Francis Collins made a discovery more important in his own life than any scientific achievement credited to him. And he, like such unparalleled scientists as Wernher von Braun and Sir Isaac Newton, believes that one does not have to choose between science and God, but that the two are compatible.

"I found great joy in being both a scientist studying the genome and a follower of Christ," he says.[10] And in light of overwhelming scientific evidence of evolution, Dr. Collins states, "In my view evolution might have been God's elegant plan for creating human-kind."

"I become, I am born, to come into being."
—THE ORIGINAL GREEK DEFINITION OF *GENOME*

VOICE OF CONSCIENCE = INNER COMPASS

"The voice of conscience," as Dr. Collins describes it, is another way of saying we are governed by an *inner compass*, an innate nudge to do the right thing.

Think, for a moment, of the many ways your inner compass

provides you with hidden impulses, day in and day out, warning you to stop—to avoid danger—or urging you to bravely step out of your comfort zone to do something He has intended you to do.

And any mother who has awoken in the middle of the night sensing that she needs to check on her child knows that your inner compass even works when you are asleep.

HOW DO I KNOW IT'S GOD'S VOICE— NOT MY OWN?

A mother on a playground, in the midst of a cacophony of children, can recognize the cry of her own child above all the others. How is that possible? It's part of our built-in inner compass system.

In the Bible we are told that the voice of God is not heard like a great wind, earthquake, or fire, but that He speaks in a "gentle whisper"[11] or "still small voice."[12] That means you shouldn't expect to hear God speak to you in a booming Gregory Peck–like voice. Instead, your inner compass will be communicating to you in much the same way that you receive instinct or intuition.

Undoubtedly, your personal desires will sometimes try to trump the "still small voice" with your own human reasoning. The best way to test a counterfeit—whether it's God's voice you are hearing, or whether it's just your own—is to always return to Step One: Talk to the Navigator. Pray. If you are wrestling with a difficult issue, turn to the Bible. No matter what issue or circumstance you are wrestling with, the Bible will help direct you. By putting your attention on the words and wisdom of the ancient scriptures, clarity often emerges that surpasses all understanding.

Here's a story that illustrates how two people who never met, and were separated by thousands of miles, on different continents, were Divinely Aligned as the inner compasses of their GPS directed their paths.

HEROES TO EACH OTHER

"You will die here. You will never see home again."

The sweat-faced North Vietnamese guard with rancid breath menacingly spat hateful words at Leo Thorsness.

The prospect of seeing home again was, in truth, the strongest inner motivator keeping him going during six years of unimaginable incarceration.

It had been on April 30, 1967, seventy miles from Hanoi, that an enemy missile struck Leo's F-105 Wild Weasel aircraft and caused it to explode.

"It felt like we'd been smacked by a sledgehammer," he recalls.[13]

The canopy flew off and he ejected at ten thousand feet—a distance seven times higher than the Empire State Building—at a speed of about seven hundred miles an hour, a hundred miles an hour faster than the maximum speed recommended for F-105 ejection.

"My helmet ripped off, my body felt as though it had been flung against a wall and my legs flailed outward," said the Minnesota farm-boy-turned-war-hero.

Only eleven days earlier Leo had been responsible for a heroic military action that wiped out two enemy missile sites, shot down two enemy MiGs, prevented two parachuting American pilots from being shot at by enemy planes, and saved another U.S. aircraft. For those actions he would be awarded the highest honor: the Congressional Medal of Honor.

With only seven more missions to go, he would soon have been on his way home to Gaylee and Dawn, his wife and daughter, but instead, at that moment, he was floating toward a tangled jungle on a Vietnamese mountain-side, almost certainly facing death or the horrors of becoming a prisoner of war.

In his mind, "A voice . . . rather than a thought . . . repeated like a tape loop, 'Leo, you are going to make it!'" *That* was an inner compass. He said later, "It was the first time I had a prayer preemptively answered." In other words, before Leo could even cry out to God, God replied.

Minutes later Leo was surrounded by a dozen stern-faced, machete-wielding males ordering him to walk . . . but he couldn't. His knees had been destroyed in the ejection.

He was taken to the notorious lockup for POWs known as the Hanoi Hilton, where his accommodations for the first three of his six years of imprisonment were spent in small solitary cells.

For eighteen straight days and nights—then off and on through-out his incarceration—the Vietcong tortured him; beat him; broke his back three times—all in the quest of getting an American officer to condemn the war.

"They bent things that didn't bend," says Leo. "At times I couldn't tell if I was screaming or imagining that I was screaming."

He felt like a failure when he finally broke. And experienced only a modicum of relief when a cell mate counseled, "Leo, in here, either you break or you die; some do both."

Almost daily the guards tried to break his spirit, to pierce the protective mental armor that Leo, with God's help, created for himself against the aloneness and hopelessness that left him sleepless many nights.

"Americans hate you. They write terrible things about you in the newspapers. They don't care about you. You will die here."[14]

Yet, on other nights, for reasons he never quite understood, he'd sleep like a baby.

Four decades later.

"Now I know why!" said Leo Thorsness, struggling to grasp the odds of an extraordinary godwink that was unfolding right before him at a baseball stadium in Texas.

Jane South Ellis stared at her hero, the man she'd prayed for every day at sixteen, never in the world thinking she'd have an opportunity to meet him in person, let alone at a stadium seating fifty-five thousand people, at an event she'd at first resisted attending.

Thirty-nine years earlier, in 1971, Jane was a bubbly, energetic cheerleader when she and her teammates each wore a small metal bracelet bearing the name of a prisoner of war. They pledged to wear it until that POW was released from captivity. Etched into Jane's $2.50 bracelet was the name LT COL LEO THORSNESS 4–30–67.

"I wore my bracelet every day for two years," says Jane, thinking back on her teen years in Mount Pleasant, Texas. It was an integral part of her youth.

"Every Wednesday we wore our bracelets to a youth meeting at church and prayed for our POWs. I prayed for the safety and well-being of Colonel Thorsness every night."

A year or so later the boy she'd been dating in her senior year, John Ellis, went off to college ahead of her and came home one weekend proudly showing her his own bracelet. It had the name of a missing-in-action soldier, "MAJ. GREGG HARTNESS 11–26–68."

This seemingly small gesture further deepened her love for the man she would soon marry.

With great clarity Jane recalls the day in 1973 when she and her parents stood before a television set watching the return of Colonel Thorsness, who had been released from captivity.

"I jumped and said, 'That's him, that's him. That's my POW, Colonel Thorsness!'"

That evening she removed the bracelet that had been a part of her accessories for two years, placed it in a box in her bedroom, and thanked God that her prayers had been answered. She penned Colonel Thorsness a note expressing her gratitude for his safe homecoming, sent it to an address provided by the military, but never received any response.

The bracelet was placed in a cedar chest with other keepsakes, all but forgotten for some forty years.

•　　•　　•

Again, fast-forward—to June 2010.

"Tell 'em we can't go." Jane sighed through the cell phone to John, now her husband of thirty-five years.

With an exaggeratedly plaintive tone he replied, "How often do we get free tickets to an Astros game? Let's go. It'll be fun."

"Oh, okay," she relented.

Once she got to Minute Maid Park, Jane felt better about coming to the game. There was an excitement in the air. It was a nice evening and folks seemed to welcome a break from the economic woes of 2010. The mingling of popcorn in the air with the comical antics of the organist that came over the loudspeakers hyped the adrenaline of the crowd.

Seated on the third deck of the stadium, Jane and John chatted with their friends and watched the Jumbo Tron projection of the ceremonial first pitch. It was a routine event. Some distinguished person would go toward the mound, throw a pitch to the catcher, then take a seat in the private box of the owner behind home plate.

Jane watched and nearly burst as the announcer, in a booming voice, introduced the white-haired man who was walking onto the field: "The Houston Astros are honored . . . that the first pitch for tonight's game will be thrown by an American war hero, and a former prisoner of war, Congressional Medal of Honor recipient Colonel Leo Thorsness!"

The crowd cheered. But no one was louder than Jane. Excitedly she bounced, shouting, "That's my POW. That's my POW!"

Instantly from within, the voice of her inner compass urged her to take an action, to step out in faith.

"I've got to meet him," said Jane, turning to her husband with a furrowed brow, her mind racing to figure out how she could do it.

"Well, he's sitting down there with Drayton McLane," said John, looking at the big screen, watching the colonel take his seat next to the Astros' owner. At this stage of his life, John was fully compliant . . . he understood that when his lovely wife set her mind to it, few things were impossible.

"I'm going down there," she affirmed, with determination.

The distance from the third deck to home plate was considerable and studded with obstacles—official people strategically stationed to prevent her from getting to her destination. At each entry point Jane animatedly poured out her story of the cheerleader who wore the POW bracelet of the man who'd just been up on the screen. The youthful gate attendants shook their heads, most asking, "What's a POW?"

"Why don't you try the fan accommodations office?" said one official, trying to be helpful.

There, Jane repeated her story—that she just wanted to meet her hero—but encountered the same wall of resistance.

"The fan accommodations office is not very accommodating," Jane complained to John and her friends when she returned to her seat.

How can I possibly get to meet Colonel Thorsness? she repeated—never thinking that she was actually uttering a prayer—a communication that was being transmitted to, and was overheard, by the Navigator of her own GPS—God's Positioning System. And that He was, in turn, communicating back to her via an inner compass, and a godwink that was about to happen.

Just prior to the start of the fifth inning, Jane's prayer was answered; her godwink delivered. As is almost always the case, God answered her prayer—to Divinely Align her with others—in a way she would have never expected.

A camera crew and a young woman came up to Jane's friend in the seat next to her and introduced themselves as Astro marketing representatives. Soon they were broadcasting an interview on the big screen, telling her friend, and the entire stadium, that she'd been selected to receive twenty-five thousand dollars if an Astros player hit a grand slam in the sixth inning. The crowd cheered.

As the camera crew began to move on, Jane seized the moment, stepping out in faith again. She quickly introduced herself to the marketing representative and rapidly repeated the story about the sixteen-year-old cheerleader who wore the POW bracelet of a man who, at that very moment, was seated down there in the owner's box.

"Do you know how much I'd like to meet him?" Jane asked pleadingly.

"Oh! My grandfather was a POW. I think we can make that happen," said the young lady, authoritatively flipping the security pass hanging around her neck. "This pass gets me anywhere in the ballpark."

Jane was soon following the young woman past one gatekeeper after another—many of whom had previously blocked her—arriving at the final, most secure checkpoint outside the owner's box, just as the seventh-inning stretch was about to begin.

The final gatekeeper was older than herself. *Thank goodness*, thought Jane, *at least she'll know what a POW is.*

From her vantage point Jane could see Colonel Thorsness. She watched as the attendant whispered to Mr. McLane, who then spoke to the colonel . . . watched his face lighten, his eyes widen. He straightened, jumped up, and briskly came up the steps, taking them two at a time.

"You had *my* POW bracelet?" said the colonel, approaching Jane with open arms and an astonished countenance.

She nodded quickly as tears began to form.

"I was a cheerleader," she said, swallowing her emotions. "You went with me everywhere. You went to the football games with me."

"Did we have a good team?" he joked, to deflect his own emotion of the moment.

"Yes, you even went to the prom, but . . . the most important place you went with me was to church."

The sincerity of her words seemed to strike the war hero in the heart; he struggled to force back his own tears.

"It was a very unpopular war," he said thoughtfully. "The guards repeatedly told us, 'You will die here.'"

"I prayed for you every night," interjected Jane with a tight throat.

"Many nights we couldn't sleep. But other nights, we slept like babies," said Colonel Thorsness, pausing a beat. "Now I know why."

There was a moment of silence. Perhaps a moment of honor for the awe each was feeling in that millisecond; somehow, among all of these thousands of people, against all odds, these two individuals, who had an invisible thread of connection, had just been, by God's grace, connected.

> " . . . Somehow, among all of these thousands of people, against all odds, these two individuals, who had an invisible thread of connection, had just been, by God's grace, connected."

"You are my hero," said Jane softly.

"No," Colonel Thorsness sighed. "You are my hero."

Jane South Ellis's story was so astonishing that she felt the need to share it with everyone she could. After all, what an extraordinary godwink that Colonel Thorsness, who lives in Huntsville, Alabama, would be divinely aligned on God's Positioning System to be in the same baseball stadium, containing thousands of people, in Houston, Texas, on the same day and time that Jane was reluctantly placed there.

A little more than two weeks later Jane was retelling her story over dinner at the home of their son's future in-laws in Fort Worth.

Jill, the mother-in-law-to-be of Jane's son, pensively listened. "That's so interesting," she said, adding, "You know, I went to school in Fort Worth with a girl whose father was MIA . . . missing in action." She paused, slowly shaking her head. "It was so sad. Her mother never remarried, never heard anything about her husband, until 2005 . . . his remains were sent back."

Jane looked at Jill sympathetically, then asked, "What was his name—the MIA?"

"His name was . . ."—she searched her memory—". . . Gregg Hartness."

Jane and John looked at each other.

"I have goose bumps! Major Gregg Hartness. That's John's MIA," shouted Jane.

The awareness struck her like a bolt of lightning. She was astonished at how the inner compass of her life, like a magnificent tapestry, was being woven right before her eyes—stitched together with the life of Colonel Thorsness—and her husband, John—and now her son's mother-in-law-to-be, and Major Hartness. Jane's life was being divinely aligned in an unbelievable way.

Holding her husband's arm, she burst with excitement; "In nineteen days we both got the end to our POW and MIA stories!"

WHAT IF I DON'T GET DIVINE ALIGNMENT AND GODWINKS IN MY LIFE?

Surely some will read how Jane Ellis was divinely aligned with Colonel Thorsness through godwinks and think, *Well, that's nice that she received them, how come I don't?*

Here's a promise: You *do* receive godwinks. You *do* have Divine Alignment. All the time.

You are like a radio. The Navigator may be transmitting, but if you don't plug in and tune in, you'll never receive His messages.

One of my readers once made this crystal clear to me. "Godwinks happen when you *allow* them to happen," she said.

YOUR TAPESTRY

Our take away from the Jane Ellis/Colonel Thorsness story is that each of us has a similar tapestry; our lives consist of threads woven from one person to the next—people we've met in the supermarket line, at our kids' school, or at church—and as we influence each other, each thread contributes to the tapestry of another.

Maybe you have felt that such experiences are just accidental encounters, and you've been willing to let life take you where it takes you. Alternately, perhaps you feel that you've been in control, with your hands, and your hands alone, on the steering wheel of life.

May I suggest another perspective?

Pull back and view your life in a long shot—from above—revealing the patterns that emerge, noting that so many of your so-called accidental meetings with people are much too precise and auspicious to fall within the parameters of reasonable probability. And that other external forces must be guiding you, placing you in such Divine Alignment.

Expanding upon that thought, follow the intertwining threads of events in the life of Hollywood screenwriter Dan Gordon and others in the next story.

INNER VOICES, INVISIBLE THREADS— IRENE'S STORY

"I heard the mother's agonizing screams . . . saw an officer make a flinging movement with his arm and something rose into the sky like a fat bird. With his other hand he aimed his pistol and the bird plummeted to the ground beside its screaming mother, and the officer shot her too. But it was not a bird."[15]

Dan Gordon, Hollywood screenwriter, sat in his car, riveted by the powerful images that were being delivered by the sweet voice with a foreign accent coming from his radio. The voice belonged to Irene Gut Opdyke, a compellingly articulate Polish Catholic grandmother who was describing the horror and hate she had witnessed. She'd relocated to America after World War II and was telling Dennis Prager's Los Angeles radio audience the extraordinary story of how she, as the housekeeper for a Nazi commander, was able to hide twelve Jewish people in the basement of the commander's villa—literally under his nose—for nearly two years.

Any listener would have marveled at how this strong-willed woman, fortified by an inner compass of compassion and steel, had put her own life at risk for the benefit of others.

Hanging on every word, Dan had just "happened upon" Dennis Prager's program while driving home, and there he remained, in the driveway, to the end. The scenes of a compelling screenplay were unfolding in his mind, more unbelievable because they were fact not fiction.

I have to find her—I need to hear her whole story, pledged Dan.

He phoned the radio station the next morning. "Give us your number and we'll pass it along," said the producer.

Awaiting a callback, Dan considered the odds: *Was it just an accident that he'd tuned in to that particular station, at that time, and "just happened" to hear Irene? Or was it something more—some kind of alignment that could only be described as divine?*

"Hello, honey." The voice through the telephone made him feel like he'd known her forever.

That was the first time Irene said "Hello, honey" to Dan Gordon, but it wouldn't be the last. It was the start of a fifteen-year relationship so close that Dan would consider her to be like another mother.

He would become inextricably involved in her life, driving her to speaking engagements, helping her protect the rights to her story, and, in her later life, providing the kind of assistance that would have come only from a son.

Over the years, Dan tried in vain to get a film made. He was equally unsuccessful in convincing a television network to do a Movie of the Week on the life of this remarkable woman. Finally, he landed backers for a Broadway play called *Irena's Vow*. With a powerful lead performance by Tovah Feldshuh, it received extraordinary praise from audiences.

• • •

A pivotal crossroad in Irene Gut's story occurred when, as a young nursing student living far from home, she was chased by advancing Russian troops.

"This is hard to say," she wrote later. "I was seventeen. I was shy with men; I had never had a boyfriend, never been kissed, I was a good Catholic girl. The Russian soldiers did not shoot me; they caught me and beat me unconscious. Then they raped me and left me for dead in the snow."[16]

Swept along by the swift-moving torrents of Hitler's war, she found herself enslaved, working in a German munitions factory for no wages. One day she collapsed from chemical fumes and exhaustion.

"You are jeopardizing the efficiency of the factory; you are too sick to work," reprimanded the commander, a major in the SS named Rugemer.[17]

Terrified by her knowledge that weaker members of the Polish population would often simply "disappear," she begged him to let her continue working.

He took pity, and assigned her to work in the dining rooms of the officers' quarters near the munitions factory, adjacent to a fenced-in ghetto incarcerating members of the Jewish population.

Through a rear window, Irene witnessed more horror. More hate.

"Behind the barbed wire stood hundreds of people whose yellow stars marked them as Jews . . . bewildered and frightened, the black-uniformed SS men sorted them roughly." Then gunshots rang out.

Driven by an unmistakably clear inner voice, Irene made a decision that "could have brought me a bullet in the head." She sneaked out daily to slip food under the fence of the ghetto.

"I did not ask myself, 'Should I do this?' but 'How will I do this?' Every step of my childhood had brought me to this crossroad; I must take the right path or I would no longer be myself.[18]

"One's first steps are always small," she added. "I had begun by hiding food under a fence."

Irene followed her inner compass.

While waiting tables in the officers' quarters, she overheard the head of the Nazi SS say that "the Führer wants all the Jews exterminated" and that soon the Nazis would begin removing Polish Jews who were working at the officers' quarters. She began to plot to save her coworkers.

By then, Irene was trusted by the commander, who also employed her as his housekeeper. When Major Rugemer revealed that he was moving to a large villa and he wanted Irene to oversee the transition, she knew her opportunity had arrived.

"When I went down to the basement of the villa I felt stirrings of excitement," said Irene. "It was so elaborate . . . a kitchen, a bathroom and servants' quarters. Several people could easily live down here."[19]

It couldn't have been more perfect. The villa had previously been the home of a wealthy Jewish architect who, it was later discovered, had built a secret tunnel leading from the basement to the garden.

Still, it would be a few weeks before the workers finished painting and preparing the villa. Irene had to wait for them to leave.

She advised her Jewish coworkers of her plan. "We've been praying for something like this," whispered one friend. "God has heard us."[20]

Yes, but will I be able to carry out my plan before the SS comes to snatch them away? wondered Irene. *How will God allow me to transfer them to the villa without getting caught?*

Divine Alignment, as it usually does, auspiciously unfolded with extraordinary godwinks. The next morning, when Irene's boss greeted her as she arrived for work at the officers' dining hall, he said, "I forgot to tell you, we won't be serving dinner tonight. There's a concert in town, and then a party. Nearly everyone from the plant is going."[21]

That evening, when the officers' quarters were vacant, Irene led her Jewish escapees to a temporary hiding place—a large duct above the bathroom that was adjacent to the major's bedroom suite.

She was nearly caught when an SS officer, searching for Jews, confronted her, but he backed off upon learning that she was Major Rugemer's housekeeper.

The next night, after Irene had fussed and cooed over the hung-over major, getting him to bed with a glass of milk and a sleeping pill, she stealthily led her wards to their new home, in the basement of the major's villa, shortly before he took occupancy.

For many months Irene sneaked food and clothing to her twelve hideaways, who had created elaborate warning systems and were careful to prevent any noise from revealing their hiding place. She frequently performed her clandestine activities while lavish parties were taking place upstairs, parties that were often attended by the head of the SS.

One afternoon, basement dwellers Lazar and Ida Haller nervously told Irene that they needed to speak with her. They confessed the most shocking news—that Ida was pregnant.

This was a dangerous predicament. A crying infant could expose the twelve in hiding, plus the baby and Irene—that was fourteen people who would most certainly be put to death. They pleaded for her to provide the necessary items to abort the baby.

"No," said Irene, forcefully reflecting her strong beliefs and following her inner compass. "No. You must not think of it. Do not let them take another life!"[22]

She reasoned that they should wait—not do anything—that the war might be over soon.

"Hitler won't have this baby," she reiterated firmly.[23]

Yet Irene was on the threshold of another crisis.

The major came home early and discovered two of Irene's stowaways, upstairs, helping her in the kitchen.

"Herr Major!" cried Irene when she saw him.

He was furious.

She pleaded for the lives of her friends.

He turned and angrily stormed out.

That evening he returned, in a state surly drunkenness.

"I'll keep your secret, Irene," he snarled. But as he advanced toward her, she knew the favor came with a price.

"Do you think I'll keep your secret for nothing?" he slurred.

"Major Rugemer, please . . ." she pleaded, with frightened eyes, feeling revulsion rising within her.

"I want you willingly, Irene. That is my price."[24]

Tears welled up in her eyes as he took her hand and led her up the stairs.

Shame and humiliation haunted Irene for years.

"It was worse than rape . . . I knew I had to bear this shame alone," she later wrote. "I could never tell my friends how I had bought their safety. Their honor would never allow them to hold me to this bargain."[25]

The only good news was that each day the war with the Russians moved closer, and that was one day closer to Irene's release from bondage as the major's mistress, and hope for her friends in the basement.

That day finally came. With the roar of mortars and gunfire within earshot, Irene was able to smuggle her group in a horse-drawn hay wagon to a woods, where they made their escape. To be certain that they would go, and not insist that she accompany them, she concealed the truth: she lied that it was safe for her to remain behind, because "underneath, the Major was a good man, that he 'helped us keep our secret.'"[26]

The war had rendered Poland a nonexistent country, divided between Russia and Germany and then pulverized and plundered by both. Irene believed there was no home to go home to. She feared that her Polish family could not have survived.

She considered migrating to Israel. And when the Jewish Historical Committee became aware of what she'd done on behalf of so many Jews, they treated her as a heroine and were only too willing to be of help. But before she could depart, a case of diphtheria, at the last minute, kept her behind.

At the time it seemed nothing more than a twist of fate. But, in hindsight, Irene would learn that Divine Alignment was again working its way in her life.

A UN delegate from the United States was conferring with a rabbi at the camp where she was staying. During their introductions he asked to hear her story. At the end he extended a hand and said, "The United States would be proud to have you as a citizen."[27]

"America?" she asked.

"America," he replied, with a smile.

Time passed.

In New York, Irene found work in the Garment District and began rebuilding her life.

One day she was sitting in a cafeteria near the UN. A man came by. There was one seat available, next to her.

A godwink was about to occur.

"You look familiar," said the man. "My name is Bill Opdyke."[28]

In moments the mystery was solved. Bill Opdyke was that UN delegate who had said, "The United States would be proud to have you," and who facilitated Irene's migration to the United States. They began to see each other. And, as love stories go, they courted, married, moved to Southern California, and had a little girl named Janina; anglicized, Jeannie.

"I was a fourteen-year-old freshman in high school when the phone call came during dinner," said Jeannie. "My mom got up from the table to take it. I could hear her voice raising."

"What's she talking about?" she asked her dad, startled to hear her mother speak that way.

"She's telling her story," he replied with a furrowed brow, comprehending that secrets were becoming exposed.

When she finally came back to the table, Irene tried to explain, through tears, that the call was from a young college student who was researching his thesis. His premise: that the Holocaust never happened.

"Never happened? What could a student possibly mean, that the Holocaust never happened!"

Jeannie was confused by her mother's passion and anger. She had never heard the word *holocaust*. Her mother had never talked about her life during the war.

"What is it, Mom? What happened?"

Irene firmly looked at her husband and daughter with an expression of shock, overwhelmed by the sudden revelation unfolding in her mind. "All this time I've kept silent, I've allowed the enemy to win. If we don't speak out with the truth, history can repeat itself."

Not sure what to say, Jeannie and her dad put their arms around Irene as she continued to weep.

"I've no choice," she said with resolve. "I have to tell the truth."

"There was a godwink the very next morning," says Jeannie.

Her dad was the president of the local chamber of commerce; he received a call after breakfast that the speaker, scheduled for that day, had to cancel.

"My dad turned to Mom and said, 'Irene, here's your chance. Would you like to share your story?'"

She did. She was highly nervous, and worried that her accent might prevent people from understanding her, but she did it.

A reporter was in the audience. He wrote the story.

"It snowballed from there," says Jeannie.

Soon Irene was speaking frequently. Rabbis called her to speak at synagogues. And she received many requests from schools. She especially liked letting young people know the truth about the Holocaust.

At one event a couple asked Irene if her sisters were still alive. She said she didn't think so.

"We're going to Poland, we can look for your sisters," they volunteered.

Irene dismissed the offer. She didn't take them seriously.

Weeks went by before Irene heard from the couple again.

"They had taken the names of Mom's four sisters, went to the town where Mom was born," says Jeannie. "People remembered the Gut sisters, but didn't know where they might now live, or if they were even alive."

Jeannie said they tried everywhere, including the embassy. No luck.

"On their way to the airport, back to the States, the couple stopped at a small corner store—a mom-and-pop kind of place. As the husband was buying snacks, the couple took one last stab at their mission. Pulling the list from his pocket, the man asked, in a loud voice, if the shopkeeper knew any of the names. Before the shopkeeper could reply, a woman shouted from the back of the shop. *"That's me!"*

The woman ran to the front of the store.

"It was my mom's sister," says Jeannie.

The sister was given Irene's address, and within hours, a telegram was sent.

Irene was overcome with joy. "That was my telegram from heaven," Jeannie remembers her mom saying, many, many times after that day.

"Less than a month later we got her tickets to go to Poland," Jeannie says.

At the time, at about age sixty, Irene still had more surprises to come.

When she went back she reunited with many old friends,

including her wards in the basement of the villa, Lazar and Ida Haller. She then met their son—the baby who was conceived in the basement of the villa, whom Irene refused to allow to be aborted—now a young man named Roman.

"This is the baby that lived only because of you," they said.

"Roman and Mom hugged," said Jeannie. There were tears.

But the most startling news was yet to come. Irene learned that after the war, Nazi Major Rugemer had become ostracized and home-less, shunned by nearly everyone.

Lazar and Ida Haller, in a remarkable display of compassion—perhaps the kind of compassion they learned from Irene—offered to take him in. After all, they reasoned, Irene had said that "underneath, the Major was a good man, that he 'helped us keep our secret.'"

Roman, as a child, had fond memories of the major; he recalled, at age five and six, calling their houseguest "grandfather."

Looking back, Jeannie says, "The phone call from the college student was truly a divine appointment. We never got his name, never heard from him again, yet the timing was so profound for him to call at that time and shake my mother up . . . to unloose those memories and for her to see the importance of speaking out on what happened."

In 1982 Irena Gut Opdyke was named by the Israeli Holocaust Commission as one of the Righteous Among the Nations, a title given to gentiles who risked their lives by aiding and saving Jews during the Holocaust, and was presented with Israel's highest trib-ute, the Medal of Honor, in a ceremony at Jerusalem's Yad Vashem holocaust memorial.[29] Unlike other righteous gentiles, who were Protestant, including the names of Schindler and Bonhoeffer, Irene Gut was Catholic.

Irene died in 2003. She never was able to see her story drama-tized six years later, on Broadway. But Dan Gordon the playwright brilliantly unfolded a portion of Irene's life onstage. And, at the end of each performance, after Tovah Feldshuh took her bows, Jeannie Opdyke Smith, Irene's only daughter, surprised the audience by walking onstage, telling some additional stories—many incredible godwinks—reaffirming for each theatergoer that what he or she had just seen was real. It really happened. More important, in the words of Irene, "We cannot let history repeat itself."

Dan Gordon misses her. "I had never encountered that kind of goodness, purity, and innocence. Her goodness was at a level that was staggering. She didn't think about it."

Irene Gut is a powerful example of what one person can do. Under circumstances more trying and horrendous than most of us could ever imagine, she always listened to the inner voice of God within, through daily conversations with the Navigator, and she always followed the invisible threads of her inner compass.

The truth of how we are guided by an inner compass was further exemplified in another episode in Dan Gordon's life, a story about his son, Zack.

ZAKI'S PLAN

Five-year-old Zaki Gordon was waiting for this moment. His dad was finally calling home from Israel, where he'd been working on a film.

"I made up a movie," Zaki chirped excitedly into the phone.

"That's wonderful, I can't wait to hear it when I get home," said Dan.

"But I have to tell you now," Zaki insisted.

"I want to hear all about it when I get home," Dan replied patiently, "but long-distance calls are very expensive."

"I have to tell you now."

"All right, if you can tell me *why* you can't wait till I get home, and it makes sense, you can tell me now. But if not, you've got to wait till I get home, okay?"

"I can't wait because I don't know how to write yet. And by the time you get home, I might forget it. So I have to tell you now!"[30]

Dan Gordon, seasoned Hollywood screenwriter, had just been trumped by the superior reasoning of his first grader. And, for the next forty-five minutes, as unseen calculators clicked off an accumulation of intercontinental telephone charges, he listened to Zaki's movie pitch. After which, he thanked and praised his boy, called his agent, and asked for a meeting with Steven Spielberg's development person at Amblin Studios upon his return to the States.

The day of the meeting Zaki anxiously awaited his father's arrival back home.

"Did they like it?" he blurted excitedly.

"They loved it. Steven Spielberg's company wants to make your movie." Dan was beaming.

"They do?"

"Yes."

"Cool," said Zaki.

"Let me give you their notes."

"Notes?"

"Yes, things they want to change in order to make the movie."

"But," said Zaki with a thoughtful look, "if they change it, it won't be my story anymore."

And so it was that Dan Gordon attempted to explain to his very bright, highly creative child the facts of Hollywood life. After a long, reasoned, and spirited discussion, Dan picked up the phone to his agent and said, "Tell Amblin we don't have a deal. My partner won't agree to the changes."

It was no surprise to anyone that young Zack Gordon excelled in school and went off to higher education at Columbia and NYU—without once revealing his grades to his parents, contending that grades were an imperfect measure of performance. Only when it was time for graduation did his parents discover that he was summa cum laude.

For a short but sweet period thereafter, Zaki and his dad were both working in New York, Dan on the production of his movie *Hurricane* and Zaki as a production assistant for an HBO film. Over treasured dinners in Greenwich Village, they'd have long talks, like colleagues as much as father and son.

Zaki expressed his dislike for the backstabbing that goes on in university departments and for unimaginative curricula, and his frustration with policies that forbade students from getting their hands on cameras until they were upperclassmen.

"If I could start my own film school," he once said with excited gestures, "I wouldn't have all those separate classes. I'd have one big class: *Movies—Everything You Need to Know!* This class would be total immersion in filmmaking."

Only weeks later, when the Gordon family gathered in Los Angeles for Hanukkah, there was a tragedy beyond comprehension. Zaki's young life was extinguished.

Attempting to enter the heart and mind of Dan Gordon in order to discern even the smallest inkling of the pain he must have endured upon learning of Zaki's instant death when his car collided with a fuel truck is utterly impossible.

There are no words to describe the depth of agony a parent endures when a child leaves this earth ahead of him.

When you lose a loved one, you begin to think about the meaning of life itself. After asking all the "why, why?" questions, you wonder about the afterlife, and whether your lost loved one has now reconnected with other souls that have gone on before.

Dan thought about "Papa" and his mother, Goddess . . . yes, that was her name. He missed them dearly. He missed hearing Grandma

Goddess read stories to the children at bedtime in a delightful ritual that included hot chocolate with a marshmallow on top and a cookie. He missed hearing his father's voice with his Russian Jewish accent.

Dan reflected that his father was not only Zaki's grandfather, but also his godfather, meaning, "that he was responsible for Zaki's spiritual upbringing, indeed for his soul."

Dan was amused when he remembered how, for some reason, his father had insisted that he was born on the first day of Hanukkah in 1898, not 1895, which was generally known to be the truth. And, even when he discussed his eventual death with his son, Papa said, "Ven it comes time . . . you put it down like I'm telling you: 1898."

Therefore, when Papa died, Dan ordered the gravestone engraved with the year 1898.

"What are you doing?" exclaimed Goddess. "Your father was born in 1895."

"What do you care?" replied Dan, with a slight smile. "He wants 1898, we'll give him 1898." And then, mimicking his father's accent: "Dat's de vay it's got to be."

It never made sense . . . until . . . Dan and the family stood in the cemetery for the unveiling of the stone for Zaki. It was then that the godwink struck them like a bolt of lightning.

It turned out that Zaki had died on the anniversary of his grandfather's entrance into the world, the first day of Hanukkah. And Zaki's death had occurred exactly one hundred years to the day after his grandfather's birth—1998 versus 1898.

The point of this story is to illustrate how we each receive impulses from an inner compass. And it is up to us to respond to those nudges in order for the Divine Alignment that has been planned for us to unfold.

Exemplifying that point, one year later, Dan boarded a plane bound for Calgary, Canada. He slipped into a seat next to a woman.

They began to chat. The woman said the reason she was traveling was to research a Calgary project; the city had built a cultural park, and in the community in which she lived, Sedona, Arizona, they were doing the same. She went on to explain that it had been decided that the cultural park in Sedona would include a film school, but the planners were stymied—they didn't know what kind of school would attract students.

Dan looked at the woman. He was experiencing one of those powerful impulses we can receive from our inner compasses. For an instant he felt like he was playing a role in a movie, one whose screenplay had been written not by him but by someone else, and he couldn't wait to find out the ending. In reality he was correct in his feeling. The "screenplay" was *not* written by him, but by *Him*.

Before the plane touched down in Canada, Dan told his seatmate how his son Zaki Gordon had a brilliant vision for a one-class curriculum: "Movies: Everything You Need to Know." He described Zaki's plan for one big class, class size, equipment lists, budget, everything that his son had envisioned.

Dan's inner compass had not only directed him to engage in conversation with a stranger on an airplane, but within months he found himself moving to Sedona, immersed in the creation of the Zaki Gordon Institute for Independent Filmmaking.

Today, to state its mission, the school manifesto uses Zaki's own words:

> If you want to find the next wave of filmmakers, you don't need to look at those working their way up the ladder in Hollywood or even those making shorts at USC, UCLA, or NYU. Maybe look at the kid on the corner with the video camera . . . kids . . . with stories to tell.[31]

Working shoulder to shoulder with Yavapai College president Dr. Doreen Dailey, cofounder of the Zaki Gordon Institute, Dan has helped to nurture the school's evolution, and he draws immeasurable joy from the faces of graduates who are beginning exciting new chapters in their lives, each taking with them a little piece of the spirit of his boy Zaki—a spirit that lives and breathes in the hallways and editing rooms of the school.

"Do you know why I've been such a proponent of this school?" Doreen once asked Dan.

He shook his head.

"I had a rough childhood, filled with challenges. But there was a man who inspired me, became my mentor, and who pushed me to achieve academic excellence, to get my BA, my master's degree, and eventually my doctorate. I would have been nothing without his guidance and love."

Dan listened attentively, wondering where her story was leading.

"One of the reasons I'm such a supporter of the Zaki Gordon Institute is because that man's name . . . is Zack Gordon."

Dan couldn't have been more stunned by being hit by a two-by-four to the side of the head. "Try to calculate the odds against the utter perfection of that design—i.e., Divine Alignment—and you'll go insane," says Dan.

Yet, a while later, the odds became even more preposterous.

"It was opening night in New York for *Irena's Vow*, a very significant night," recalls Dan, "and during dinner with one of our most important backers, I received a call on my cell phone. When I looked at who was calling, I saw that it was one of Zaki's closest friends, whose wedding I had just attended the weekend before. I thought it might be important to take the call."

"Guess where I am," said the newlywed.

"I know where you are—on your honeymoon," replied Dan.

"Right, our honeymoon in Alaska. But, at this very second, I am standing in front of the Zack Gordon Youth Center in Juneau."

Instantly Dan's memory put the pieces together: *Juneau. That's where Dr. Doreen Dailey had grown up—that's where Zack Gordon had influenced her youth.*

No wonder she was so drawn to the Zaki Gordon Institute.

Dan went back to his dinner with his Broadway backers, shaking his head and smiling at the cascading godwinks of ongoing Divine Alignment.

WHY, WHY?

Perhaps, notwithstanding these amazing godwinks, you are still struggling with the tragic loss of Zaki's life, asking yourself why a loving God would allow such a bright light—this creative, articulate, budding young filmmaker—to be extinguished so horribly.

No person on this earth—not the wisest person you know—can authoritatively answer that question. It remains an unsolved mystery.

But, we *can* make some suppositions.

Suppose God sees things from a wider perspective than you and I. Imagine that we are like ants at the bottom of a giant redwood tree in the midst of a great forest while God, from above, can see everything with great clarity. If that's the case, would it not stand to reason that something that doesn't make sense to us, way down here in the weeds, actually makes perfect sense to God, as He sees it, as part of His perfect plan?

Are you still with me?

Therefore, from God's perspective, things that we call horrible may be viewed quite differently.

Take death. It's the worst thing that can happen to us, and to our families.

But, what if God considers death on earth as simply "graduation" to the next life that He has in store for us?

And remember, at graduations, the graduate is excited about moving on to the next level; those who feel sadness and regret are those of us who are left behind.

If you accept this supposition as a possibility, then consider what

God can do by graduating one of His children—in this case, Zaki—sooner than we would have desired. Subsequently, through the inner compass of his dad, God was able to implant the idea of building the Zaki Gordon Institute, allowing Zaki's spirit to prevail, touching the lives of many thousands.

WHAT SHALL WE CONCLUDE FROM THIS CHAPTER?

We each have an inner compass. The question is . . . do we listen to it? And do we question it with the Navigator? In each of the preceding stories, individuals were clearly guided by an inner compass toward outcomes that were nothing short of amazing:

- Acclaimed scientist Dr. Francis Collins was goaded by a grandmother into listening to a question from his inner compass: "Does a scientist draw conclusions without considering the data?" That led him to evaluate the question "Is there a God?" as a scientist, without bias. And that quest led to discovering great joy in being *both* a scientist and a follower of Christ.
- The inner compass of Congressional Medal of Honor winner Colonel Leo Thorsness convinced him that he would survive and played an integral role in carrying him through six years of brutal incarceration as a prisoner of war, while the inner compass of a sixteen-year-old cheerleader caused her to pray for him incessantly . . . demonstrating the power of prayer for each of us. Ultimately, the cheerleader's inner compass provided the impetus for the two to meet in a fifty-five-thousand-seat stadium.
- The inner compass of screenwriter Dan Gordon nudged him into a meeting with Irene Gut, resulting in a fifteen-year

friendship, but also in his becoming a key ally in helping her to reveal a extraordinary story of bravery—a story in which she followed her own inner compass to save twelve Jewish people from death, including a baby who, except for her convictions, would have been killed.

- Dan Gordon was again led by his inner compass when a stranger on an airline caused him to move to Arizona to oversee the development of a film institute fashioned after the ideals of his son who was tragically killed.

QUIET VS. LOUD VOICES

Our inner compass is that quiet, still voice that is often drummed out by the loud external voices all around us, the often overbearing yet well-meaning voices of family and friends who try to redirect our paths to fit *their* comfort zones.

Do you remember when you were a child looking into a star-filled sky? You said, with wide-eyed innocence, "I wish I may, I wish I might, have this wish I wish tonight . . ."

Then what happened? One of those loud, well-meaning voices issued a command: "GROW UP!"

Your confidence began to erode. Your positive outlook cross-faded into cynicism.

You had no way of discerning that those adults around you were imposing their own fears on you. They quashed your dreams because they, most likely, had failed to have the confidence to reach their own. They didn't even realize that the words of their well-meaning but misdirected counsel was extinguishing a flame within you.

Yet the loud voices don't always belong to others. Sometimes it's your *own* loud voice that overpowers your inner voice. Fear and anxiety may be rising up inside you like a monster emerging from a tar pit in one of those old black-and-white movies; you find yourself running amok, going in circles.

These are the times on your journey through life when you need to pull over to the side of the road. Pause. Take a deep breath, and return to Step One: Talk to the Navigator.

It's amazing how a quiet, prayerful conversation with your Navigator can create a peace and clarity that surpasses all understanding.

> And the peace of God, which surpasses all comprehension, will guard your hearts and your minds in Christ Jesus.
>
> PHILIPPIANS. 4:7 (NASB)

It's never too late to reach for the volume control. To turn down the loud, annoying voices from others or yourself. And to turn up the still, small voice within. You *can* have your dreams.

GPS STEP 2

LISTEN TO YOUR INNER COMPASS

Each of us has a factory-installed compass, often called instinct. Tuning in to and listening to your inner compass is often the most important directive you can follow.

MAPPING
YOUR DESTINATION

As the Cheshire cat said to Alice, in Wonderland, "If you don't know where you are going, any road will take you there."

The events in our lives are not random. Instead, we each come into this world with our destiny built in. But, because God has given us free will, it is up to us, as individuals, to program ourselves to determine what *we believe* that destiny to be.

Through Divine Alignment, He will continually place opportunities, events, and people along each of our paths to help get us to where we need to go. But, if we sit by the side of the road waiting for our destiny to come to us, what happens?

Nothing.

Your destiny will not arrive in a limo to pick you up.

Determining *where* you want to go in life is your job.

And once you do—once you pull yourself from the curb and head in whatever direction your inner compass is telling you to head—the signposts will unfold . . . godwinks, all along the way. That's a promise.

I want to share a story about a woman who came from meager

means, who envisaged what she wanted, mapped it out in her mind, and went for it.

CAROL BURNETT'S DIVINELY ALIGNED MAP

Do you ever look at a performer like Carol Burnett and say, "How did she have it so easy? How'd she get all the breaks? How come I can't be as lucky?"

"Your destiny will To be in Carol Burnett's shoes, you may need *not arrive in a limo* to trade in your parents for a mother and father who didn't have two dimes to rub together and *to pick you up."* had difficulty even tolerating each other—not because they weren't fond of each other, but because there were so few days they were sober enough to even stand up. That's why they weren't together. And why Carol was primarily raised by her stern but loving grandmother, Nanny, living in a boarding-house in an impoverished area of Hollywood.

Yet, even in the most trying circumstances, God pierces the darkness with light. Attending Hollywood High School, Carol displayed a natural sense of humor. She had personality. And she believed in herself.

While working her way through UCLA, she received her first big laugh from an impromptu line she delivered in a college play, and this instantly refocused her aspirations, causing her to change her major from journalism to theater.

"They laughed and it felt great. All of a sudden, after so much coldness and emptiness in my life, I knew the sensation of all that warmth wrapping around me. I had always been a quiet, shy, sad sort of girl and then everything changed for me. You spend the rest of your life hoping you'll hear a laugh that great again."[1]

From that moment on, she made a map for herself, complete with a schedule. To reaffirm it, she told others, including her boyfriend Don, exactly what she planned to do after college.

"I had it all worked out. Finish out the year, get to New York some way, make my Broadway debut, marry Don, and make enough money not to care about how much money I was making. That way I could take care of everybody I loved and have enough to give to needy people and never tell them who did it."[2]

Of course, the real question was, how in the world could she save up enough money to get to New York?

Nanny told her, "It could take years."

Yet, "I wasn't worried . . . I 'saw' myself in New York, and I saw it happening very soon," says Carol.

Shortly after that, Carol and some classmates were invited to a private party by the head of the UCLA Music Department to perform scenes from a show they were doing

The crowd loved it.

As Carol and Don mingled during dessert, she was greeted by a mid-fifties couple, whom she later identified as Mr. and Mrs. C.[3]

"You have a pretty loud voice, there," said Mr. C, with the air of a businessman.

"Thank you," said Carol.

"What do you want to do with your life?"

"Pardon?"

"This? Do you want to do this?"

Carol smiled shyly. "Yes, I think so, yes, very much."

"Well, why aren't you?"

"Pardon?"

Don came to the rescue. "All musical theaters are in New York."

"So, go to New York . . . why don't you go now?"

"Money," said Carol, as evenly as she could, looking Mr. C directly in the eye.

"How much will it take you to get to New York?"

"Oh, a thousand would be nice," she replied, barely regretting her flippancy.

"It's yours."

Gulp.

Mr. C handed her a card and told her and Don to come see him in La Jolla the following week.

"Well, when are you coming down here?" said Mr. C into the phone when Carol called ahead for an appointment.

"Friday?"

"Be here at nine a.m. sharp." He hung up.

Carol had actually mapped the path she wanted to take. And that path went from L.A. to New York. Was this the door of Divine Alignment making it possible for her to fulfill her dream?

On Friday, Mr. C the businessman sat behind a large desk. Carol and Don nervously sat across from him.

"His black eyes were positively piercing," remembers Carol.

"Well, we made it," said Carol, brightly and awkwardly.

"*Why* do you want to do this?" inquired Mr. C, picking up where the conversation left off from the week before.

"Because I'll never be happy doing anything else," reasoned Carol, thinking, *Wouldn't everyone think that way?*

"What makes you think you'll succeed?"

"I don't think it. I know it," asserted Carol, amazing herself with the simplicity and confidence of her statement.

"Well, I think you might have a good shot at it," concluded Mr. C. "I'm going to lend each of you one thousand dollars. You can pay it back in five years. No interest. I want you to promise to use the money to go to New York. It's enough for a ticket . . . and stretch out the rest until you can find a job."

He buzzed his secretary, who brought in two checks, already made out.

Carol and Don thanked him repeatedly and started to get up.

"Wait a minute."

They sat back down.

"There are stipulations. Aside from this being a loan, you cannot tell anyone my name." (Thus "Mr. C.") "Also, when you do make it, you have to promise me you'll help other people out . . . like I've helped you. Got it?"

He began looking at some papers on his desk. "Good-bye."

Carol and Don stood and walked toward the door. Over her shoulder she gave Mr. C a promise: "We'll make you proud."

"I hope so. Good luck."

Six weeks later, at a farewell party some friends threw for Carol and Don, someone shouted, "Hey, Burnett, what's gonna be your first Broadway show?"

She didn't miss a beat, responding pointedly, "A musical. George Abbott will be the director!" Abbott was the most admired, most successful director of the day.

I wonder, does this remind you of *Alice in Wonderland's* Cheshire cat . . . *If you don't know where you're going, any road will take you there?*

Still amazed with how her recently articulated career map was now beaming her from Los Angeles to New York like a character in a science-fiction movie, by "just happening" to encounter Mr. C at that private party, she couldn't help but wonder, *Will my first Broadway show really be a musical . . . directed by George Abbott?*

How many struggling actors are there in New York? We might have the answer to this question if we could calculate the exact number of waiters and waitresses in the city. The Big Apple attracts theatrical wannabes from every corner of the planet, with a mysterious appeal to live like church mice on scraps left over from meager incomes.

As Carol's "map" continued to unfold, it was speckled with Divinely Aligned people who helped move her along toward what she believed to be her destiny. Someone told her about a residence that was partly underwritten by wealthy Park Avenue ladies who wanted to help young actors. It was called the Rehearsal Club. Every day the twenty to thirty girls who lived there would go off on endless rounds of disappointing auditions before taking them to their jobs waiting-on-tables.

They all wanted an agent. But they quickly learned they needed credentials from prior theater work before they could *get* theater work, and that no agent would take them on unless they could get that work. They'd all slap themselves against the head and say, "How is this possible?"

But one agent *did* have a word of advice for Carol. "Put on your *own* show," he said.[4]

She took him seriously, rounded up twenty members of the Rehearsal Club, and staged a two-night revue at a run-down theater that they were able to rent by pooling one hundred dollars a night.

They invited scores of agents, reviewers, and some well-known actors, two of whom—Marlene Dietrich and Celeste Holm—actually showed up and were sitting in the audience.

Backstage, Carol spoke with the Navigator. "This is it. If they don't like me, I'll quit, so please God, make them like me."

She received three curtain calls and lots of bravos, plus a terrific review in *Show Business*, leading her into a one-year contract with the William Morris talent agency. She was Divinely Aligned with another agent named Mr. Willi, who didn't have the clout of William Morris, but whom she decided to sign with, one year later, after learning that *having* a William Morris agent didn't mean he would actually go out and get you work. Even though Mr. Willi hadn't been representing her during that period, his door was always open, always available for advice.

One day, a highly discouraged Carol Burnett sat before Mr. Willi. She explained: After a short burst of attention from the Rehearsal Club revue, things had stalled. She was still waiting tables. He gave her a pep talk, told her to keep plugging. And suggested she work up some new material for auditions.

As she was leaving Mr. Willi's office, she had another auspicious godwink. She met a man in the waiting area who introduced himself as Ken Welch, a writer who had seen her perform at an audition; his comments also encouraged her that day. He handed her a card.

A few weeks later Carol called Ken to ask for help in developing some special material for a New York cabaret gig that Mr. Willi had booked for her at the Blue Angel. Ken came up with a life-changing idea. It was the height of the Elvis craze and he wrote a sketch about a young girl going gaga over a rock star. Except, instead of Elvis, this girl was nuts about John Foster Dulles, at the time the anything-but-sexy, always-grumpy-looking secretary of state.

The auspicious Divine Alignment of Carol Burnett and Ken Welch produced a showstopper at the Blue Angel, and soon she was invited to perform on a stream of television shows, including *The Ed Sullivan Show* and NBC's *Jack Parr* while the *New York Times* did a tongue-in-cheek editorial about the political ramifications of the song she sang in the sketch.

During an appearance on *Meet the Press*, Secretary Dulles added fuel to the buzz about Carol's sketch. He was asked, "What's going on between you and the young lady who sings that love song about you?" The secretary replied, with a twinkle in his eye, "I make it a policy to never discuss matters of the heart in public."[5]

But Carol continued to learn that every UP has a DOWN. Conversely, every DOWN has an UP.

She finally got the *big* call: to audition for a revival of Rodgers and Hart's *Babes in Arms*, which would open in Florida, prior to going to Broadway. *Ah, finally,* she thought, *a Broadway audition with promise!* That was the UP. It wasn't a show directed by George Abbott, as she had envisioned, but it would do.

Standing on an empty stage, next to a pole with a naked lightbulb, holding a script with shaking hands—you know the scene; it's been reproduced in a dozen films—she nervously auditioned for unseen faces sitting in the dark.

Please, God, don't let me lose this, she prayed silently.

This is a good time to remind ourselves that just because we clearly articulate to the Navigator what *we* want in life—what we *desperately* want and desire and have given up everything for—He doesn't always see things from our pea-brained perspective. We are bobbing in a rowboat on the ocean. He sees the whole ocean. He also sees the ship just over the horizon that we should be on, instead of on the rowboat.

Carol began the audition. Instinctively, she knew her performance was way below her capability. In fact, it was her worst reading ever. She blew it.

That was the DOWN.

But—and I've set you up for this *but*—God's ways are not our ways. His plan will unfold in ways we usually cannot foresee.

Had Carol, at that moment in time, been able to transcend her terrible disappointment at blowing the audition and see the puzzle pieces on the table of her own life, she would have appreciated God's outlook.

In hindsight, she had failed to get the Broadway-bound Rodgers-and-Hart show for a very specific reason. It wasn't her destiny.

That audition was like a puzzle piece that seemed to fit, but when it was put into place, one would instinctively know that jamming it together wouldn't do any good.

Seen from God's Positioning System, Carol would have understood why the Rodgers-and-Hart show was not for her. Because that very evening she received another telephone call. This one was from someone inviting her to try out for a different play, based on the Hans Christian Andersen fairy tale, "The Princess and the Pea."

It would be an off-Broadway musical called *Once Upon a Mattress*. Directed by George Abbott![6]

Wahoo!

Five years after she had facetiously told friends at her going-away party that her first Broadway show was going to be a George Abbott musical, *she got the part*, and the rave reviews that went with it!

And, on the exact due date, five years to the day since Mr. C gave her the one-thousand-dollar loan, she sent him a certified check, paid in full.

She saw Mr. C only once after that, years later. He had not responded to any of Carol's occasional notes to him or acknowledged receipt of her check. This puzzled her. It turned out that she was able to meet him and Mrs. C for lunch. He was no longer the brusque businessman she had known, but a graying man who spoke much more quietly.

"Did you receive my check?" she asked.

"Yes, and you were right on time."

Later Mrs. C took Carol aside and cleared up the mystery of his failure to acknowledge her check.

"He's so proud of you. He's too embarrassed to tell you that he never answered your letters because he didn't want it to look like he was trying to take credit for your success."[7]

On parting, Carol hugged Mr. C. After all, he was one of the most important godwinks, Divinely Aligned, in her life.

Into his ear she whispered, "Thank you, Mr. C., for giving me my start."

"You're welcome," he said.

She smiled at him. She had—as she had once promised—made him proud of her.

A short while later she learned that Mr. C had died.

WHAT ABOUT THE OTHER PROMISE?

No, I didn't forget. Carol promised Mr. C to throw the rope over the wall *to help others*.

In one way, this was evident to all of America for eight years, at ten o'clock every Saturday night on CBS. That was when a huge portion of the country sat down to watch *The Carol Burnett Show*. If you had the good fortune to be in the audience, think about it. Have you ever seen another show like it? No. There's never been one.

That's because Carol Burnett, week in and week out, exemplified how she gave a helping hand to a regular family of actors—including Tim Conway and Harvey Korman—and then had the grace to get out of the way and allow them to garner more laughs, much of the time, than she did. That's what a star does.

And behind the scenes, there were dozens of other stories of how Carol Burnett made it a practice of extending a helping hand to lift someone up.

Let me illustrate with a story about a girl who eventually became my wife.

SHYNESS AND SADDLE SHOES

"She was the shyest child that ever sat on my lap," says Miss Phelan, Louise DuArt's third-grade teacher. "I would lift her chin up and say, 'It's okay, you can look at me.'"

In junior high, Louise was still shy.

"I was the shy, dorky girl in saddle shoes." She adds, "The last one to be chosen for a team in gym class, but eventually, I found an escape: I learned to pretend I was other people."

She wasn't kidding. The more Louise imitated the odd-sounding math teacher or the low-voiced crossing guard, the more laughs she got from other kids. She started coming out of her shell. When she did impressions of movie stars like Katharine Hepburn or Barbra

Streisand, her schoolmates were fascinated. And when kids got the idea that she could imitate their mothers and maybe get them out of school by telephoning, she became downright popular—no longer "the dorky girl in saddle shoes."

Louise perhaps had no conscious notion that she was actually starting to map her path in life—heading for what she believed to be her destiny—but she was doing exactly that by trying out for school plays, reading movie magazines, and hanging with other kids with artistic inclinations.

Most important, she never missed her favorite Saturday-night TV show starring Carol Burnett and those wacky sidekicks Tim Conway and Harvey Korman. She'd study the range of characters that Carol came up with every week and try to imitate how her heroine changed her voice to become Eunice, a regular character on the show.

She had no way of knowing it, but there were many parallels between her and Carol Burnett. Like Carol, she had been a shy child, from a family that constantly struggled to get by, and like Carol, she was instinctively mapping a future for herself. She imagined herself performing on *The Carol Burnett Show,* and shared her vision with others. And similar to Carol, who received little encouragement when she told her grandmother her "big ideas" about going to New York and becoming a star, Louise never held her breath to hear an "atta girl" at home.

Louise's mom, Grace, was a lot like Nanny. You never had to tap your toe waiting for her to deliver an opinion on any topic, from politics to boyfriends. She told you. Straight out. Yet, under all the bluster, there was a heart the size of Texas, full of love.

Grace was a strong Catholic believer. Every week she'd give Louise a quarter and send her to the Our Lady of Good Counsel Church, in Quincy, outside of Boston, to light a candle to pray for the souls in purgatory.

Louise figured she had just one prayer. A quarter's worth. So she'd drop the coin in the box, light the candle, fold her hands tightly together, and say, "Please, God . . . I just want to meet Carol Burnett."

Does God hear the prayers of a little girl?

Well, it usually doesn't happen overnight like in an old black-and-white movie. Louise didn't bump into Carol Burnett at Filene's Bargain Basement, and her heroine never showed up in the audience of one of her school plays. In fact, as far as Louise was concerned, nothing happened at all. Still, she refused to dim the desires of her heart, and kept on praying that along her pathway she'd one day meet the star of her dreams.

When a friend in Los Angeles said she ought to leave Quincy and move out west, offering a place to stay until she got on her feet, Louise sold her car, bought a plane ticket, and again pressed toward the mark, willing herself toward what she believed was her destiny.

She wormed her way into Los Angeles Community College even though she wasn't a California resident, and soon was hanging with the drama-class kids. She jumped at the chance to be in a school play and, unbeknownst to her, positioned herself for a key Divine Alignment. By stepping out in faith, heading toward her goals, she was giving herself the opportunity to become visible to someone who could help her.

One evening after a performance a man in the audience came up to her and told her that the Krofft brothers were casting a touring show based on one of their Saturday-morning TV shows, *H.R.Pufnstuf*. The lead character was Witchiepoo, an overexcited witch with a green face and a long nose with a wart on it, played by Billie Hayes.

Louise had no idea what roles might be available, but every Saturday-morning-TV-watching kid at the time knew Witchiepoo, so she made a cassette tape recording of herself imitating Witchiepoo, and headed for the Krofft brothers' studio.

Sometimes just having the gumption to show up in a place where you don't think you have a ghost of a chance of becoming visible is when God allows you to be seen.

Somehow she was ushered into the office of Sid Krofft.

She was still terribly shy, comfortable only in hiding behind a character voice, as Sid asked her about herself.

She quietly told him she wanted to be a performer.

"Do something for me," demanded Sid.

"Ah, well . . . can I play you something?"

Sid looked confused. Louise pulled her cassette player from a bag and hit the play button. Her impression of Witchiepoo filled the room.

"That's Billie Hayes, why are you playing me that?" demanded Sid.

"It's not Billie Hayes," said Louise, modestly. "It's me."

"That's you?"

She nodded.

"Wow. It sounds just like Billie."

The moral of the story: Figure out *where you want to go*. Map a path—fully understanding that you may need to take many different routes to get there. Prepare, to the best of your ability. And boldly step out in faith, heading for what you believe to be your desired destination.

For the next several years Louise traveled with the Krofft brothers, performing in multiple shows, including the role of Witchiepoo in all the road shows.

Somewhere along the line Louise found herself cast in a TV show that called for her to imitate her heroine: Carol Burnett. With uncanny ability, she even imitated Carol's trademark Tarzan yell.

From God's perspective, way up above the puzzle pieces on the table of Louise's life, perhaps everything was now in proper position for a Divinely Aligned godwink.

Why would it take so long? Perhaps He needed the time—several years—to get all the people, events, and geography in place to answer the prayer that little girl once uttered, weekly, at a Catholic church in Quincy, Massachusetts.

A producer who worked with Carol somehow saw a videotape

of Louise's impression of the star. She thought it was a scream, happened to be on her way to see Carol, and took it along.

A short while later, out of the blue, Louise's phone rang. It was *her*—Carol Burnett! The superstar was reaching out to lend a helping hand—inviting Louise to come to the Disney Studios for lunch.

Can you imagine the joy she must have felt?

"It was the most wonderful day of my life," says Louise. "I teared up when I met her . . . and we gabbed like old friends."

When Louise left the studio she looked to the sky and said, in a loud whisper, "Thank You, God!"

As an afterthought, she added, "Now, God . . . if I could just meet Tim and Harvey."

Little did she know that that afterthought was another communication to the Navigator; her request was being placed on the to-be-answered list.

It took ten years. But another call came in. Totally unexpected, it was Tim Conway. Completely unrelated to Louise's meeting with Carol, the classic comedian said, "Harvey Korman and I are thinking of taking a show on the road, featuring sketches from the *Burnett* show. We'd like to know if you'll join us."

You could have knocked Louise over with a feather!

Tim later explained: "Someone sent me a big stack of tapes. I took the top one off the pile, watched it, called in my wife, Charlene, and said, 'What do you think of her?' She said, 'Great,' and I said, 'She's the one.'"

Do you recall my earlier question: "Does God hear the prayers of a little girl?"

Talk to Louise.

For over a decade she's costarred onstage all across America with Tim Conway—and until he died, Harvey Korman—playing to sellout audiences.

In hindsight, her pathway has emerged into a clear picture of *cause and effect*.

She mapped it.

COMMON DENOMINATORS: CAROL, LOUISE

I hope it's obvious by now. There are very clear parallels between these two women. And you should take heart from each of their stories, because no matter how difficult your circumstances are, you, like them, can reach what you believe to be your destiny.

Carol and Louise came from low-income households, each experiencing considerable degrees of difficulty. Carol grew up in a family that was rendered quintessentially dysfunctional by alcoholic parents. Louise was reared in a low-income home and slipped into other people's personalities in reaction to the shyness that gripped her.

Yet, in each family, there was someone—a grandparent or a mother—who was a taskmaster, from whom a steady beam of love poured.

Carol and Louise each had no idea how they could get from their meager beginnings to the big dreams they had in their heads. Yet each was undeterred. Each pressed forward as if they *knew* they could make it.

And each had a map. Carol and Louise each visualized the map, and shared it out loud with others, making themselves subsequently accountable—i.e., if they didn't follow through, and try their hardest, they could potentially lower their esteem in the eyes of the people in whom they'd confided.

They each spoke with the Navigator. As a result, their strategic placement on God's Positioning System was always pointing them to their destinations.

What makes you any different from Carol or Louise?

If they could get where they wanted to go, why can't you?

WHAT IF I DON'T HAVE ANY IDEA OF WHAT DIRECTION TO GO IN?

Just start *going* . . . pick a direction and try it. Eventually you *will* know. Your GPS will help you tune in to the direction that feels right. As with any journey, you may need to recalculate many times along the way, but get going. God can't help you if you choose to remain idly by the road.

PATH POWER

As you place the palms of your hands around the steering wheel of life, heading for what you believe to be your destiny, you simply cannot underestimate the power you hold. The choices you make, the paths you take, are everything.

Andy Stanley is a young pastor who built a vibrant church in Atlanta with some fifteen thousand weekly followers. As people came to him seeking counsel over the years, he began noticing a common theme. Whether their issues were financial, relational, or career oriented, they often concluded by saying, "I don't know how I got to where I am."

Stanley would say to himself, Hmm. *That's pretty obvious. It's the path you chose.*

In his book Andy explains, "The principle of the path is that *direction*, not intention, *determines our destination.*"[8]

When you set off in pursuit of your destiny, you are filled with good intentions. But in the end, it's not those intentions that get you where you want to go; it's the direction of the paths you chose.

As you grip the steering wheel of your life to begin your journey, you have a full tank of high-test free will—the God-given brand. *You* have most of the choices. *You* can choose to take paths that are slippery, crooked, and dark, or you can elect to travel the high, dry paths that run straight, and in daylight.

You have Path Power.

It seems so simple. Yet the consequences are profound.

OF COURSE THERE WILL BE BARRIERS

Don't be mistaken. There will be many obstacles. Many enticements for you to get off your pathway, to meander on the side roads, or even to become lost.

But usually they will not be involuntarily taken detours—you'll look back and realize that you had choices at every crossroad, a point when you could choose to travel by light, or by dark.

LIGHT OR DARK—YOUR CHOICE

The choices we make are often as simple as the decision to cross the middle line in the road. From light to dark. Or dark to light. Forces on both sides will always be tugging at you. Which side you stay on is up to you. Your free will. Your choice.

When you were a teenager, the forces of darkness coaxed you to do things you innately knew were wrong. Someone persuaded you to try alcohol, drugs, or casual sex that you knew, from deep inside, would draw you into a darker place.

Perhaps you didn't realize the darkness right away. Or perhaps the darkness made you curious; *just try it, just once.* You were literally being lured into dark places—dark bars, dark alleys, dark rooms.

As the forces of darkness tempted and tantalized you with promises you innately knew were not to be trusted, you still had your hands on the steering wheel of your life; it was your choice to take that path in the dark—or you could swerve to the light.

And if you did take the darkened path, you also began choosing to live in the shadows *of your mind*—with secrets. Things you didn't want to tell your parents, your friends, your partner, your boss, because, whether you admitted it or not, you felt shame. Darkness always produces shame. And secrets.

Each of us is given the choice. We can choose the paths we take. As Andy Stanley said, "Direction, not intention, gets us to where we want to go." Who picks the direction? You do. Will your lofty intentions get you there? Nope. Getting off your baggage, heading in the right direction, will.

And, all along, it will be your choice; the path in the dark. Or the one in light.

> People loved darkness rather than light because their deeds were evil.
> For all who do evil hate the light, and do not come to the light, so
> that their deeds may not be exposed.
>
> JOHN 3:19

GPS STEP 3

MAPPING YOUR DESTINATION

Determine the direction you believe your destiny is taking you. Write it down. Make choices to travel by light. Go.

UNSHACKLE
YOUR BAGGAGE

One of the all-time-great children's books, one that has inspired each of us, is *The Little Engine That Could*.

Through the years we've pictured ourselves trying to emulate the spirit and tenacity of that little storybook engine—taunted by others who questioned the little engine's ability to actually pull a trainful of toys to awaiting children on the other side of the mountain. We became inspired as he reached way down inside himself to find the belief, the commitment, and the persistence to get the job done.

Haven't all of us, at one time or another, seen ourselves as *The Little Engine That Could*?

I now want to suggest a new character for you to emulate: "The Little Boat That Should."

Just like this little boat, you *should* be out there on the wide-open seas, cutting through the waves, exuberantly tacking this way and that, with your sails billowing in the wind. Like the Little Boat That Should you deserve to splash for joy, heading for destinations you've always wanted to go.

But . . . you can't.

You can't because you're tied to the dock. Worse, you've lashed *yourself* to the posts. You've bound yourself with things that prevent you from setting sail—impeding God from moving you forward.

You are shackled by your own baggage.

God has people and events standing by in ports all along your future journey—at the ready to be Divinely Aligned with you—helping you get to your destiny.

But casting off will be up to you.

MADEA'S MAIN MAN

Tyler Perry is Hollywood's fifth highest paid man, says *Forbes* magazine. Yet merely a decade earlier, he was homeless, adrift, and fiercely holding on to a deep-seated resentment and anger about his father's abuse of him during his childhood.

He happened upon a simple piece of advice seen on Oprah Winfrey's show: keep a diary of daily thoughts and experiences.[1] Taking the challenge, he wrote to his Navigator with biting, self-deprecating humor, pouring out pain and anger. Eventually, his letters to God became a bridge to forgiveness and a catharsis for healing.

In hindsight, it is clear to Tyler that his diary was the key to unshackling himself from the baggage that anchored him to his past, and thereby allowing God's ignition to move him forward through a series of incredible godwinks. And what he perceived as a long bridge to cross turned out to be little more than a footpath.

Here's what happened.

One day Tyler sat down to review his letters and concluded that they'd make an interesting play. He called it *I Have Changed*. Well, he *thought* he had changed. But if truth be known, he'd released his anger toward his father, forgiven him . . . then reeled that anger back in.

"In 1992 I put together the money for the play," says Tyler. "But only thirty people showed up. It was a miserable failure."

I Have Changed opened and closed. Once again Tyler was dead broke, living on the streets of Atlanta, sleeping in his car and seedy hotels.

Yet instead of abandoning his faith, Tyler expanded his conversations with the Navigator. He became more involved with his church and continued to persevere.

Six years later he raised the money to reopen the play.

"My mother kept telling me to get a good job, with benefits, and when I opened the play again, I said to myself, 'This is it. If this doesn't work, I'm listening to my mother.'"[2]

But what had truly changed within Tyler Perry was that *this* time he had honestly let go of all of his baggage, all his resentment toward his father and others. This time he sincerely forgave them.

The play opened with no advance ticket sales. His hopes plummeted. Earlier images of only thirty people in the audience haunted him. He cried out to God, "What more do I need to do, I have forgiven everyone."

He added: "God, I don't know what you're doing, but I praise you anyway."[3]

He then sensed a voice within: *Look out the window.*[4]

When he complied with the voice, Tyler saw a line stretching around the theater. And for weeks thereafter, he saw the same line: the play was a hit.

Today Tyler Perry has catapulted the characters of his series of plays into a string of hit movies centered around Madea, a forceful, salty, maternal character with steely inner values whom he himself plays.

Like most of his characters, Madea is a product of Tyler Perry's past. She was inspired by his mother and his aunt Mayola.

"My mother is the wisdom of Madea, but my aunt Mayola, that's her wig, that's her voice, and that's her gun in the purse."

FORGIVENESS, A GIFT WRAPPED FOR YOU

Tyler Perry's story proves that forgiveness is not a gift you give to others. It is a gift you give yourself.

His father and friends may have benefited from Tyler's act of forgiveness, but it was Tyler himself who received the joy of unshackling himself from the tortured thoughts that had imprisoned him.

"If you don't truly forgive, you hold yourself back. You need to forgive so that the Father can forgive you," he says.[5]

One of Tyler's colleagues in the Hollywood writing community, actress and screenwriter Carrie Fisher, captured the concept nicely: "Resentment is like drinking poison and waiting for the other person to die."[6]

FAMILY TIES THAT SHACKLE

"My mother-in-law Edith and I were best of friends," says Carla Cooper. "But when her son and I were divorced, many things were said; choosing up sides was unavoidable, and layers of resentment made it just too painful to stay in touch."

Carla moved away. Eventually she married again.

Still, she kept warm thoughts about Edith tucked away in a corner of her heart; she missed her, and thought about her every once in a while.

One Christmas, Carla decided to take an action step. She sat down and wrote a letter.

"I told her how much her friendship meant to me. How much I missed her. And I asked her to forgive me for hurting her son and family."

Carla never received a reply, assuming that Edith got the letter and threw it away.

Some six years later she and her husband were watching a television show about archaeologists excavating in Israel.

"I told my husband that my former mother-in-law, Edith, always wanted to go on an archaeological expedition," says Carla. "And I again wondered aloud if she'd ever gotten my letter, and what she might have thought about it."

Her husband sort of shrugged and agreed that Edith had probably dismissed it.

That night Carla couldn't stop thinking about Edith; she went to bed wondering, *Does she ever think of me?*

The next day was Good Friday. And it sure was good.

When the phone rang, Carla's husband answered it, calling out that an "old friend" wanted to speak with her.

"I couldn't believe it when I heard Edith's voice on the phone. She said she'd opened a desk drawer and there was the letter I had written years before. She had saved it, hoping that one day she would be brave enough to call me."

Edith told Carla how much she had missed her, and that she forgave her.

That night Carla said, "Thank You, God," before slipping off to sleep.

Fact is, Carla had unshackled her baggage six years earlier when she wrote the letter to Edith. She released all resentment at that time. And, from God's point of view, she released that baggage, even though Edith had not.

Edith waited, getting up the courage, finally reaching out and accepting Carla's peace offering.

Of this we can be fairly certain: by unshackling her resentment, and releasing the baggage of the past, Edith also had a good night's sleep.

RELEASING YOUR RESENTMENT BALLOONS

Imagine yourself a child in a park holding the strings to a batch of helium balloons. Each balloon has a name on it. Someone who has wronged you, betrayed you, angered you, and toward whom you've carried a long-simmering resentment. Each balloon is tugging, pulling at you; it's a strain to hold on. It's work.

Now speak with God. Ask Him to help to release you from your bondage of resentment by forgiving each person. One by one, say the person's name, followed by the statement "I forgive you." Then let go.

Let your mind see the balloon carrying that person's name lift into the clouds. Feel the sense of freedom and peace that comes from no longer holding tightly to a string that has been tugging to be free.

Resist the temptation to reach out and grab the string, pulling it back to you. Don't do it. Let it go. Each resentment for each person will now soar to the heavens. If justice is to be done, don't worry, God will deal with every one of them.

MY DEAR MOTHER

I was thirty-two when I finally forgave my mother.

My mother was a strong woman, a disciplinarian. When I was seven she caught me playing with matches. To teach me a lesson she grabbed my hand and opened the old pot-bellied stove. I can still picture the red-hot coals inside. I can still recall the fear I felt as she pressed my hand into the stove, against the embers.

The pain endured for weeks. Eventually, it scabbed over. And, eventually, my feelings scabbed over as well. But the pain of resentment was always lingering beneath the surface.

How could my mother do that to me? I thought, over and over, for years after that.

My mother was the type of person who spoke her mind. It troubled me that she would say such frank and hurtful things about my friends or neighbors. As a result, I became a defiant teenager. My brothers had determined that it was easier to go along to get along with Mother. But not me. I was Mr. Confrontation. More often than not, my challenges produced undesirable disciplinary outcomes, and I completely failed to persuade my mother that my position was right and hers was ridiculously wrong.

I spent considerable time making lists of grievances in my mind, holding imaginary court, in which I presented my ironclad case to the Court of Public Opinion. Surely the court would exonerate me and provide a victorious verdict. But I never got to present my case.

At the age of thirty-two I was an executive at a TV network, married, with children of my own. When I was home for the holidays, my mother said something that pushed my buttons, so I promptly packed up my family and drove off.

Then I had this twelve-second conversation with myself.

Do you love your mother?

Of course.

Does she love you . . . enough to take a bullet for you?

Absolutely!

Do you think you'll ever change her?

Nope.

Then, why don't you just love her the way she is?

That brief conversation, I later realized, was a conversation with God. And each of the questions I thought *I* was asking, were questions He was asking.

In that short conversation, it dawned on me that I was never going to change my mother and I let go of the resentment balloon that I'd long grasped. The one with her name on it. And the release was exhilarating!

My mother and I never discussed it. But from that moment on, our whole relationship changed. Her inappropriate statements about people no longer bugged me. In fact, I found myself laughing and saying, "If Neil Simon wanted to put a character like my mother in a Broadway play, he'd have to invent her. I don't even need to buy tickets." The things that previously made me angry became genuinely funny.

Instead of making lists of grievances, I found myself writing lists of wonderful things she'd done, and realizing what a powerful influence she'd been upon me—more than anyone else—right from infancy.

Did I ever discuss that horrible incident from childhood in which my hand was singed?

No.

I suspect she harbored her own guilt about that. She probably talked with God about it, seeking her own release of forgiveness. And, once my resentful feelings and behavior vanished at the age of thirty-two, she perhaps felt further released.

Maybe—just maybe—I became her favorite son.

I don't know. But, one day I plan to talk the whole matter over with her.

In heaven.

IT'S NOT ABOUT THE OTHER PERSON

Sometimes we think that in order to forgive someone, we have to confront them. The unpleasantness of acting on that thought delays us. It's understandable. If we resent someone, why would we want to talk to them about anything, let alone rake up the details of the troubling issue? It could be embarrassing. But one of the first things you'll discover about forgiveness is that it's not about you and the other person. It's about you and God.

"One . . . of the first things you'll discover about forgiveness is that it's not about you and the other person. It's about you and God."

You don't even need to talk to the other person in order to forgive them. They don't even need to know that you've talked with God, behind their backs, and forgiven them.

Yet, as you move forward in your dealings with that individual—now free from your own bondage—you'll begin to notice how things change.

I suspect that no segment of our population better exemplifies the virtues of forgiveness than the Amish, who reside in many pockets around the nation but especially in Pennsylvania Dutch country, west of Philadelphia. Sometimes the ability of the Amish to "turn the other cheek" and to forgive is beyond what most of us can imagine ourselves doing.

I want to share with you an amazing story. It's about someone you may know as the "Pretzel Lady"—Auntie Anne, founder of the Auntie Anne soft pretzel stands found in shopping centers and train stations around America. She and her husband, Jonas, can surely tell us a thing or two about pretzels, but more important, they have dedicated their lives to teaching us how to unshackle ourselves from the bondage of resentment and lack of forgiveness. These were lessons that they painfully learned themselves as a young married couple.

AUNTIE ANNE'S PRETZELED PATH

The words of her father's prayer lingered for a moment in Anne's thoughts.

"And Lord, if there is a tragedy today, help us to accept it. Amen."[7]

Perceiving the statement as a forewarning was distant from her mind. She glanced at Jonas, traded an amused smile with him, and chalked it up to another of Daddy's eccentricities.

In the morning hustle-bustle of an Amish farm, framed against the tranquil countryside of Lancaster County, strung with miles of clotheslines that seemed to wave an independence from modern appliances, twenty-four-year-old Anne Beiler watched as her darling, not-quite-two-year-old daughter scampered out the door of their trailer home, across the yard, to Grandma's house. Blond curls waving, Angie was still wearing her jammies. Anne turned and reached for the phone to prepare her mom for Angie's arrival.

Hard work, with everyone pitching in, seems to be in the genes of Amish families. Anne's younger sister Fi helped with the masonry business. Glancing over her shoulder, making sure the coast was clear, Fi backed the Bobcat out of the barn, turned, and moved forward.

The next thing she remembers seeing was frightening and confusing: Daddy running toward her, frantically waving his arms. Then, from the corner of her eye, a sight that would be forever frozen in her memory: a tiny body lying on the ground where the Bobcat's wheels had just rolled.

"Screaming. That's all I remember, horrendous screaming. *No . . . not Angie!*" remembers Anne in her recounting of that horrible moment.

In Anne's memory, everything that followed was a blur.

"The doctor looked at me with sad eyes, and said, 'There's nothing we can do.' He pulled the white sheet up over her face."

It would be several years before Anne Beiler would become known as the "Pretzel Lady," "Entrepreneur of the Year," or author of the book *Twist of Faith*, which chronicles her extraordinary life's path. No, at that moment, the young mother of two, wife of her high school sweetheart, Jonas Beiler, just dropped into a deep, dark abyss.

She sank deeply into the kind of unhappiness that most of us cannot imagine.

In the weeks following the accident that robbed the life of her sweet, sweet child, Anne spiraled deeper and deeper into her pit of despair. She cried endlessly. She blamed herself relentlessly, *I'm a bad mother*, she thought. *I was the one who let Angie run out the door, and didn't watch as I reached for the phone that day.*

She didn't even blame Fi.

"Do you hate me?" Fi asked.

"Of course not."

"Can you ever forgive me?"

"It was an accident. Of course I forgive you," replied Anne.

Today she can reflect with more clarity. "Some may find it hard to believe, but forgiveness for Fi entered my heart immediately. I never felt angry or upset with Fi on the day Angie died, and never since then."[8]

But that didn't stop her from blaming herself. And, after a while, she became embarrassed that she couldn't seem to deal with her loss. She started hiding her crying from everyone. And many things went unspoken. Unhealthy silences grew into bitterness, depression, and guilt.

"Jonas looked sad," she says, "yet, our talks about the accident came few and far between."[9]

Soon she began sleeping on the sofa, not wanting Jonas to know she cried herself to sleep every night. Brick by brick, an emotional wall began to rise between the two of them. Anne had no one she could talk to about her guilt—about Angie.

Then there was comfort.

She was kneeling, alone, at the altar in church.

"I felt a strong hand on my shoulder. I looked up. My pastor stood there, concern etched on his face. He knelt beside me. He prayed with me, his arm around me. I wept. For the first time in months, I felt comforted."[10]

When they stood, the pastor hugged her, and said, "I love you, Anne."

At first blush that was not an unusual statement for a member of the congregation to hear. Everyone in Anne's church held the pastor in complete respect and admiration.

Yet his next comment was one she immediately determined never to tell anyone. Especially not Jonas.

"No, Anne," he said, looking into her eyes. "I love you in a special way. Please call me. We need to talk."

A day or two later Anne found herself dismissing the discomfort she felt with the pastor's words and reminded herself of the feeling of peace that surged through her body as he hugged her, and the welcome sensations she'd felt in talking with him.

"Come in, Anne," he said after she knocked on the door to his office.

"I immediately felt safe," she remembers. "Pastor walked to me from behind his desk and hugged me for a long time while I cried. I couldn't believe how good it felt to talk about Angie, about the day she died, about how I felt."

As she was getting ready to leave, the pastor again made a disquieting statement.

"It's obvious to me, Anne, that you have needs in your life that cannot be met by Jonas. But I can meet them."

She nearly fled to her car, overcome with a sense of guilt and confusion. Again affirming to herself that she would never tell Jonas about what just happened.

Still, as days passed—with every moment of her life seemingly enshrouded in black, filled with hidden tears and unspoken words—she allowed her mind to revisit the sweet, caring persona of the pastor, and how he patiently listened to her anguish, and then encouraged her.

"I met with Pastor quite often," says Anne. "Usually at restaurants over a cup of coffee. I thought *maybe I imagined things . . . maybe he didn't do anything inappropriate.*"[11]

It struck her as odd when one day he became furious with her. She had just told him something she thought would be viewed as good news—would help her to recover—that she was pregnant. Why this made him angry she couldn't imagine.

Shortly after that, she remembers, "Pastor asked me to meet him farther away than usual, at the next town down the highway. We met at a diner, then he said he needed to drive me somewhere. We drove a few miles away to a motel, one of those single-story seedy-looking places. He asked me to follow him into one of the rooms . . . I was feeling increasingly uneasy and confused. Then, the door slammed behind me."

Anne knew she had now lain down at the bottom of that dark pit. As she looked up, there was no ladder. No way out. Unless she could tell someone else, right away, she would never be able to pull herself to freedom.

"When Angie died, I thought I knew despair," says Anne, "but lying there on the bed in that dark motel room, I realized despair takes many forms."

In the car, driving back, the pastor began weaving his web of entrapment.

"No one's ever going to believe you; you know that, don't you?"

In her state of total disbelief for what she had just allowed to happen, Anne thought, *He's probably right. Who would believe me? He's the respected pastor of a loving congregation.*

In hindsight, Anne says, "I know there were choices I could have made differently. Some people may wonder why I got in the car with him, why I agreed to go into the motel room, and why I kept meeting with him. I've asked myself those questions hundreds of times. What I can say is that I completely trusted my pastor and that, at the time, he was the only person who cared enough to listen to my sadness. I was broken, grieving, and extremely vulnerable."

Anne adds, "It's what can happen when people in that position abuse their power . . . they can lead people down roads they never would have gone down on their own. I discovered this is called 'abuse of spiritual power.'"

She was trapped in the web, ensnared, and couldn't imagine how to get out. All the while that the pastor was her trusted counselor, the person to whom she could tell her innermost thoughts and concerns, she never thought that he was using that intimacy to manipulate her.

Anne compares her situation to "having heavy chains of guilt and self-loathing entwine themselves around me. And when I resolved to tell no one, I locked those chains firmly on myself. Telling the truth was the key to freedom, but because I didn't know it at the time, I quickly tossed it aside."[12]

Two years later accusations arose that the pastor had acted indecently with a member of the church. Anne's family found themselves right at the center of the controversy and they were divided right down the middle. Four of Anne's brothers believed the charges and thought he should go. One other brother and two sisters, along with Anne, refused to accept the rumors.

"There were many reasons I refused to believe the rumors," says Anne. "First, I was involved with him, and I couldn't imagine he would be with anyone but me. Second, if I took the side of those charging the pastor, I was certain my own guilt would be exposed."

Deep down she knew he was probably guilty of all charges, but she wasn't prepared to come clean.

"I was trapped in a tangled web of silence and the only thing that could have freed me was my own confession. But by choosing to stay with him and remain quiet about what had happened, I allowed him to steal my voice."

When mounting evidence against the pastor forced him to quit and move to another state, she felt a sense of relief. But it was premature.

"I wasn't free from him," says Anne. "We spoke on the phone and he remained the one person I shared everything with. I still felt trapped and controlled by Pastor."[13]

It seemed peculiar, but right after the pastor left the state, Anne's sister Fi and her husband moved to the same state.

Meanwhile, Anne had an overwhelming desire to leave Lancaster

County and Pennsylvania, thinking that a new beginning in a far away place might be just the solution for her and Jonas.

Good news: a job opportunity arose for Jonas in Texas.

But, again, the reprieve from the love-hate relationship with her controller was short-lived. Before long, the pastor announced that he too was moving to Texas. Near Anne and Jonas. And soon the families of both of Anne's sisters, Fi and Becky, moved nearby.

"My initial happiness at his arrival," says Anne, "quickly turned to pain, mental anguish and the guilt that only comes from keeping secrets. Once again I found myself drawn into a web of lies, secret rendezvous, sneaking here and there. Guilt. An overwhelming sense of confusion."[14]

Finally Anne's eyes began to open to something that, initially, was very painful. But it was the very thing that gave her the clarity of thought to take decisive action about her entrapment. She started to notice that the pastor's car was parked at places next to one or the other of her sisters' cars.

"My breath would catch in my throat," she says. *Surely not*, she thought to herself. Then, slowly, she started to see the truth.

"He had been maintaining a relationship with both of my sisters the whole time, constantly driving a wedge deeper and deeper between us so that we would never find out . . . never talk to each other about it, never find freedom."[15]

Anne opened her mind to an awareness of things that she'd previously overlooked or ignored. She added up the number of times that she had planned to have coffee with Fi or Becky, yet when she arrived at their homes, they weren't there. She'd later be told that the pastor had called, at the last minute, requesting that the sister come to church to help out with one thing or another.

Finally, it was Fi who took the initiative to have open communication and asked Anne to come over for coffee. This time she was home. As Fi spoke, the secret began to crumble.

"Just mentioning the secret made me feel stronger," says Anne.

Then Fi made a bold statement: "I left him," she said simply.

An intense hope rose up in Anne, leading her to wonder, *Could I do that too? Could I regain a normal life? Could I be happy again?*

"Fi's encouragement had finally brought me to the place where I felt ready to leave too," says Anne. "I had allowed him to steal so much from me, and I'd begun realizing just how much of my life had been lost because of his abuse of power during my time of vulnerability."

She arranged to meet the pastor at a diner.

Directly and firmly she said, "I'm not going to see you again."

At first he tried to smooth-talk her. Then he lost patience. "You can't make it without me," he sneered.

Then he switched to an old tactic.

"I'll run away with you. Come away with me," he promised.

But Anne was resolved.

"He had strung me along for years with that promise," she says. "During the years after Angie's death I'd felt so depressed, all I wanted to do was get away, and it was for this constant promise that I stayed with him."

She stood up to leave and made a determined declaration.

"No, I'm finished."

He stared her right in the face and threatened, "I will haunt you for the rest of your life."

Anne turned, walked out to her car, and drove away.

"As I look back, I see God sweeping into my life and literally tearing me from the jaws of evil,"[16] Anne says with a sigh. But she could not rest. She immediately considered what she would need to say during another conversation that she'd have to have, right away: one with Jonas.

"No one else could tell him the horrible secret before I did," she said. "He had to hear it from me. I drove straight to his shop."[17]

Again, she was direct.

"You know those things you've been hearing about all those women with Pastor? I was one of them," she said, glancing away.

A look came over Jonas's face that she'd never seen before, a look of intense hurt and surprise and shock. She couldn't bear to look at it. It wasn't rage; it was deep disappointment and confusion.

"I'm sorry," she choked, amid sobs, running out of his shop.

Later she tried phoning Jonas several times, but there was no answer. She couldn't imagine what he might do.

At home that night, she finally heard his car pull into the driveway.

"Honey, we need to talk," said Jonas. "I just want you to be happy. If you want to leave, promise me one thing . . . just promise you won't leave in the middle of the night. Just tell me about it. I'll help you pack. Take the girls with you, because they need a mother."

Anne was astonished with Jonas's reaction.

"If Jonas had accused me at that moment, I would have run. Instead, his words made me feel safe, made me feel valued in an area of my life where I had always felt weak: my mothering." Jonas told her that she was valued, a good mother, and that he didn't want her to leave.

"His forgiveness took my breath away," she says, still amazed.[18]

As others in her family learned of the abusive situation into which she had become ensnared, they too were compassionate. Instead of expressing disgust, surprise, or shame, they chose grace and forgiveness.

"His forgiveness took my breath away."

"I felt totally overwhelmed and forgiven," says Anne. "That amazing grace allowed me to continue my journey back to happiness and some sense of normal life after six years of darkness and confusion."

There was, however, one person who still refused to forgive her. "That person was me," admits Anne.

It wasn't until she became Divinely Aligned with a ladder from God that she was able to climb from that part of the pit, as well.

When Jonas's mother passed away Anne went to her home to clean up and sort through things. She discovered boxes bursting with envelopes—every letter Anne had ever written to her mother-in-law.

"The letters went on and on," she recalls, "each one a snapshot of the years my mind had blocked out—so many little reminders that I'd been a good mother to my girls even when I had felt terrible about myself. I began to feel something changing inside me—I was finding the grace to forgive myself."

As others showed love, encouragement, and forgiveness, she began gaining strength.

"I know of no other more powerful life force than forgiveness," concludes Anne.

Over a decade later, Anne's twenty-three-year-old daughter, LaWonna, asked her to accompany her to a counselor's meeting. There, she made a statement that reopened the horror that Anne and her sisters had gone through as the vulnerable prey of a manipulating pastor.

LaWonna's lip quivered as she made the admission.

"Mom, he did it to me too."

As the shocking words were spoken, Anne was instantly disbelieving that the pastor could have made her innocent child a victim too.

"Total disgust blocked my mind from allowing the information to process immediately . . . then it registered. When Angie died, we mourned her death with family and friends . . . but the spirit of my four-year-old daughter LaWonna died too . . . no one brought her flowers, no one mourned."

She hugged her daughter. For a long time.

Anne and Jonas's marriage had undergone storms of monumental proportion. But they did what each of us must do whenever we take journeys through treacherous territory: They rediscovered themselves on God's Positioning System, then reprogrammed their GPS by speaking frequently with the Navigator. They prayed together about everything, allowing God to work in their marriage and every aspect of their lives.

Jonas, the great forgiver, developed a new passion, says Anne, "a desire to provide counseling for couples who were going through struggles like we went through." Jonas ran a mechanic shop by day, but used his evenings to help others, holding regular counseling sessions at their home.[19]

"God used those years in Texas to begin showing us that our purpose would be to help people in need," adds Anne.

Once the secrets came out of the closet, Anne and Jonas felt a longing to return to the peaceful countryside of Lancaster County, Pennsylvania, to reunite with family and friends after nearly a decade.

They both grew up in conservative Amish families, some members of which refused to make use of modern conveniences such as electricity. Both learned the value of hard work and the importance of family and community.

When Jonas was a child, his two older siblings worked the farm with their father while he remained inside to help two aunts who did the cooking and the cleaning. His mother was bedridden, so at the elbow of his aunts, Jonas learned baking while working in the kitchen.

Jonas and Anne became high school sweethearts. In their early years of marriage, he made a living running a body shop, a skill he used in Texas and upon their return to Pennsylvania.

Family and friends all seemed to enthusiastically welcome them home, yet Anne had a difficult time finding a job.

"I had worked as a waitress for numerous restaurants before we moved and naively thought that surely someone would remember my hard work. 'I just don't know what's wrong,' I said in desperation.

'All these people know me and know I'm a good waitress. Why don't they hire me?'"

When we ask ourselves these questions in life, don't we often discover that God has something else for us? Something better than we would have thought of on our own?

"You've got a call, Auntie Anne," said one of Anne's nieces.

A man on the phone said, "You don't know me, but I heard you were looking for work. I started a market down in Maryland at Burtonsville Farmers' Market, and need some help on Fridays and Saturdays."[20]

The main product of the man's business was soft pretzels.

Anne did such a good job that the man soon offered her the position of manager. She liked the added responsibility and enjoyed making pretzels. Her only issue was proximity. It was a long drive from her home to the Maryland farmers' market.

In another significant moment of Divine Alignment, a friend mentioned that a stand was for sale at the Downingtown farmers' market. They sold pizza and pretzels.

"I never planned on buying my own business," says Anne. In fact, "I felt fortunate just to be managing the stand I already worked at, but Downingtown was only a thirty-minute drive vs. the five-hour round-trip to Burtonsville."

On her first day at her own stand, Anne received a bouquet of flowers with a note attached.

You can do this, honey.
Love, Jonas.

"I see many common threads in my life, one of which is Jonas's never-wavering encouragement," says Anne. "He always showed total confidence in me, whether it be in skills as a businesswoman or as a mother or as a wife. Even after I disappointed that trust, he continued trusting me."[21]

Bolstered by her husband's trust and her own faith, Anne turned the distant corner of the sleepy Downingtown farmers' market into a hustling, bustling location as two conclusions began to form in her mind.

"First, I felt we could definitely make this thing work. Sales went up each week, customers seemed happier than ever, and people loved the life and energy my family and I brought to the stand. My second thought was that the pretzels we made tasted horrible, and I couldn't wait to stop selling them."

After a month of tinkering with pretzel dough, costing a considerable amount of lost inventory, she came to the conclusion that the best course of action was to simply drop the untasty pretzels from the menu and focus on the pizza, which sold well.

Once again Anne and Jonas Beiler arrived at a barrier blocking their journey. As they had learned to do in situations like this, they stopped, recalculated, and reassessed their options; they spoke with the Navigator.

"Jonas and I sat down one evening and prayed together, asking God for wisdom regarding how to make the pretzels."

Did God respond instantly?

"He didn't seem to pay much attention," Anne continues. "Our attempts got worse and worse. But, I wasn't giving God enough time. Finally, I grumbled to Jonas, 'I'm just going to quit making pretzels and we are going to take them off the menu board today.'"

"'Well,'" said Jonas, mildly, "'before you give up on the pretzels, let me try something that might work.'"

Anne laughed. "Hey, go ahead, give it a try!"

He reminded her that he used to do some baking as a kid and that his aunts taught him a few things that might work with this recipe.

Soon, Anne and her staff were astonished.

"We could all tell a difference even before we baked that dough . . . it smelled so good, and it rose in a way the other dough never did. We rolled a tray of soft pretzels and put them in the oven. After only a minute we were once again hit with the amazing smell."[22]

"Jonas, those smell great!" she said.

Jonas grinned, his eyes sparkled, and he watched as the staff tore into the pretzels like a bunch of vultures.

"We couldn't contain our amazement," remembers Anne. "The difference was completely indescribable. The new pretzels were soft and fluffy on the inside and crisp on the outside, tasted incredible, and melted in our mouths. I couldn't wait to sell them."

Even more important, the customers liked them.

"Nearly every customer would taste, stop, turn, and shake their head in amazement. By the end of that day we were selling more pretzels simply because the word had spread around the market. Business completely took off."

At closing time Anne burst into tears of joy.

"We made $2,000 today! Two thousand dollars in one day! I never dreamed of that kind of money. That night Jonas and I just laughed and laughed. We were giddy at how well our little market had done for us. And, within a week or two of the miraculous pretzel recipe transformation, people came from all around to try our soft pretzels."[23]

Anne can now see, with the clarity of hindsight, that just after she and Jonas reprogrammed their GPS by speaking with the Navigator—just a few days after they prayed together—everything changed.

"The popularity of the pretzel changed our lives almost immediately."[24]

While Anne Beiler is the person whose name is associated with Auntie Anne's Soft Pretzels, she'll be the first to tell you that Jonas was her critical partner behind the scenes.

"He was the mastermind behind the secret pretzel recipe," she says.[25]

It was their friend Emy who came up with the name of their business, recalls Anne: "Emy said, 'Why don't you just call it Auntie Anne's Soft Pretzels?,' then, Jonas went home and made a cute little sign to hang outside the shop—it had a white background with three-dimensional baby-blue letters.

"The name and the colors would stay with us for the seventeen years I owned Auntie Anne's," says Anne.

Anne and Jonas have now devoted their lives to missions that help others . . . including couples counseling. But, referring to that spring day in 1988 when the heavenly aroma of Jonas's pretzel recipe filled the farmers' market, she says, "We couldn't have imagined that in the next seventeen years we would build more than 850 locations bearing that name."

With a reminder to each of us as we travel our own pretzeled paths, she adds, "That just goes to show that in no point in our lives can we have any idea about what waits around the next bend."

In 2005, in order to dedicate their lives to creating resources for family counseling, Anne and Jonas sold the business to one of their most dedicated employees, Anne's second cousin Sam Beiler, who was faithful to Auntie Anne's Pretzels since almost the beginning.

SHACKLES HAVE NO BOUNDS

Releasing resentment and offering forgiveness, like Anne and Jonas did, is but one of the shackles you need to think about breaking in order to allow God to move you forward. There are many other matters that can keep you tied up, like a ship lashed to a dock.

Debt is another of them.

If you've had a bad credit rating, you know it can haunt you, and follow you around like old gossip. Have you ever gotten a black mark on your credit rating? Perhaps you moved to another city and you overlooked giving a credit-card company your forwarding address, thereby missing a payment? And you later learned, painfully, that it often takes seven years for that blemish to be erased from your bad reputation?

Dave Ramsey has made a career out of guiding people like you and me out of the quagmire of debt, and repositioning ourselves, with God's grace, to become unshackled from the fierce hold being in debt can have upon us.

DAVE RAMSEY'S BABY STEPS

Speaking directly to the 7 percent of Americans who live paycheck to paycheck, Dave Ramsey is the affable guy on TV who seems to always impart commonsense wisdom about protecting your financial well-being.

He has successfully graduated a million or so attendees from his Financial Peace University, a thirteen-week course taught via video, with volunteer hosts, at churches and military bases.

Dave came to his commonsense awakening after losing everything. At twenty-six he was making a quarter of a million a year, but he, like many of us, ignored his mounting debt. Dave's debt reached four million dollars before everything collapsed.

"That led me to a very uncomfortable place," says Dave. "My mirror. I came to realize that my money problems, worries, and shortages largely began and ended with the person in my mirror."

Dave Ramsey is a champion of helping people to unshackle themselves from the bonds of debt. Today he helps us look ourselves in the mirror and take a series of seven "baby steps"[26] leading us to pay everything off and cut up our credit cards.

It's simple, "biblically based, commonsense education and empowerment, which gives hope to everyone," says Dave.

DEBT AND SHAME—SQUIRE'S

Let me share with you a personal story that I've never, publicly, told anyone.

Why haven't I? Embarrassment and pride.

Those are usually the culprits that cause us to harbor things that would be healthier to get out, into the light of day. So . . . let's get it out.

When I left the ABC television network after twenty years, I didn't, as I led many people to believe, leave of my own volition. I was fired. (Yikes, why is that so hard to say?)

ABC management wouldn't have termed it that way. Like most corporations these days, they'd use a popular "euphemism"—which means a substitution for an expression that may offend—replacing "downsized" for "fired." But when it happens to you, it really doesn't matter what they call it—they both hurt.

What happened?

There was little connection between my performance for the company and the dastardly actions.

You see, ABC management had been sold a bill of goods about another executive at another network, CBS. Somehow, he had orchestrated a series of "recommendations" from very influential people, convincing ABC's top executives that they just had to have him, notwithstanding the fact that the man had been previously terminated twice by networks. And he'd previously worked for ABC. Yet they hired him—at a level that meant he was my new boss.

My history with the man was that when I was hired to be ABC's first vice president of children's television, I was brought in over him, and he, unfortunately, got squeezed out. Then he became my competitor at NBC and subsequently CBS. What's more, the mothers at Action for Children's Television, a lobbying group, often painted me as the guy with the white hat, whom they had lauded for ABC's *Schoolhouse Rock!* and the *Afterschool Specials*, while painting him—my unintended nemesis—as the guy in the black hat.

Uh-oh. Are you getting the picture? So was I. The proverbial handwriting writing on the wall was in the shape of a bull's eye. On my back.

After two decades of witnessing network politics, I sensed what was coming. As an obnoxious optimist, I woke up one morning filled with enthusiasm. *It's time for me to leave the network anyway,* I thought. *I've put in my twenty years, and it's high time I became the entrepreneur I've always wanted to be.* I shared this excitement with my attorney, suggesting a severance amount that I thought would be a fair "package" for ABC to pay me for exiting my contract after two decades of superior service. (At least, that's how it was inflated in my mind.)

My attorney wasn't so enthusiastic. He suggested I exercise caution. That I wait.

Wait? Wait for what? thought I, annoyed.

But two weeks later my expectations were realized. I was called in by the new guy—my old nemesis—and fired.

How could they do this to me? I whined, as if I'd been blindsided.

I was crushed, even though the amount of severance I thought would be generous two weeks earlier was nearly tripled by ABC's greater generosity. Notwithstanding this, it was a major blow to my ego. My pride. And, until this very writing, I've never had the guts to utter the words: *I was fired.*

Somehow, the truth represented a badge of dishonor—evidence that I had been rejected, presumably a failure.

Once I finished my temper tantrum, I put on a happy face, telling everyone I encountered that I had "decided to leave ABC" to become an entrepreneur. Which, two weeks earlier, would have been a completely honest statement.

But . . . who could have imagined that going out on my own would have been so difficult—so hard to make the transition from a regular paycheck to generating my own income? One year later I understood why the word *entrepreneur* rhymes with another word meaning farm fertilizer.

Making things worse, I had jumped into the pool of entrepreneurialism just when the television industry was going into its worst depression ever. It was the first time in the history of the business that TV networks had made less money than they had in the previous year, excepting the year when, having nothing to do with an economic turndown, the government unexpectedly pulled cigarette advertising from TV.

Every television show I tried to sell, and every producing job I pitched, hit a brick wall. I ran through my severance at ABC and was now looking at virtually no income to pay my mortgages and my family living expenses. Simultaneously, due to the depression, the real estate market had come to a standstill and I was unable to sell either my property in Manhattan or the one in Connecticut; still, the banks wanted their money. I had become a terrible credit risk, and was turned down for every loan application.

In the third year after leaving my ABC job, my total income was thirteen thousand dollars, against expenses many multiples above that. How did I survive? I'm surprised I was able to.

For reasons I still cannot explain, I even failed when I went to a bankruptcy attorney to seek relief; he said I wasn't a candidate.

I had no choice but to do the most difficult thing in the world—the hardest thing I have ever done—to put my hat in my hand, and go to friends—producers and others I used to work with at ABC—people who used to come into my corner office on the thirty-seventh floor, perceiving me to be a big-shot TV executive. I had to go to them and share my plight—to ask them for a loan.

Every single one of them helped me out. And I learned, only much later, that every single one of them, based on prior experience, never expected they would be repaid.

One of the men I went to was Joe Barbera, who, along with his partner, Bill Hanna, created many of television's most memorable cartoon characters, from Yogi Bear to the Flintstones. How embarrassing do you think it was for me to go to Joe, swallow my pride, pour out my heart, and ask for a loan?

That humbling experience was repeated five times over, all with prominent people in our industry. I felt as low as I could go.

In the fourth year after being fired, things started picking up; I landed producing assignments for syndicated shows, sold a couple of pilots, and began squeaking my income back above my costs. Then a headhunter finally came through, and I was offered a position as president and CEO of a small cable television network. I had mountains of debt, but things were getting better and I started writing my first *When GOD Winks* book.

Auspiciously, the book came out just before the tragedy of 9/11. I had fashioned it as a book of hope. It turned out America had never needed hope more.

But all along I felt like I was tugging on anchors of debt, from every direction, holding me back, including those loans from good friends. Unshackling myself from all that debt—unlashing my vessel from the dock—was something I craved.

Then, one of the happiest days in my life was when Simon & Schuster offered a significant advance for the rights to the book. And the very day the check arrived, I sat down and wrote letters of gratitude, including checks to repay my loans in full, to every one of my friends who had helped me out when I was on the rocks.

Every one of them called, with choked voices, to tell me that they had never expected to be repaid. Did they need the money now? No. They were all very wealthy people. But that wasn't the point. For them or for me.

For me, the point was that I was finally able to unshackle myself from debt and shame; I was able to make good on promises to old friends. Believe me, there is no greater feeling of joy and relief.

In hindsight, I now see the bigger picture: by unshackling myself from the debts of my past, I was enabling God to move me forward, to the happiest days of my life.

The wisdom in the ancient scriptures was never more clear:

Let no debt remain outstanding,

except the continuing debt to love one another,

for he who loves his fellowman

has fulfilled the law."

ROMANS 13:8 (NIV)

UNSHACKLING BAD HABITS

If you have a bad habit or an addiction, you can feel yourself tied to the dock—like the Little Boat That Should I spoke about earlier—making it more difficult for God to advance your lot in life. But, when you choose to unshackle yourself from that which has a grip on you, you are able to soar toward better days.

There is no end to the things that may be holding you back.

People who smoke are shackled.

People who swear are shackled.

People who practice sloth are shackled.

Some people are shackled not by their own bad habit or addiction, but someone else's. Often, family members become codependent on the addict.

Sometimes people are shackled to the past.

My wife and I had family friends, a couple with two teenage girls; the father was the breadwinner—a television personality—and his lovely wife, Mary, doted on him and her children. She cooked every meal, ironed his performance clothes and their school outfits, packed his travel bags and the girl's lunch boxes.

One day Mary's husband died. And the daughters were out of the nest at college. Mary was left in an empty house with the unfulfilling prospect that she was no longer needed; she had no purpose and identity for herself. She was shackled to her nurturing role of the past. That became her baggage until she finally cut herself loose and got a job, and satisfied her desire to serve through community activities.

Everything that holds you back is another strap around the post at the dock. The sooner you unleash it—and *you* is the operative word, for no one can unleash bad habits or baggage other than yourself—the sooner the heavens will open up, pouring down a torrent of grace that will amaze you!

UNSHACKLING FROM BAD DEALS

There may have been times when you made an arrangement for a service that you needed, or hired someone to work for you, or found someone to partner with—that at the time made sense. But over months and years, circumstances changed. Perhaps they didn't deliver the way you expected them to; maybe they let you down, or other factors came along to sour your relationship.

Still, you may be paying for their service and privately fostering resentment. You may recall what someone told you: "The devil you know is better than the devil you don't know." You avoid making a change because you're worried that you might replace the unsatisfying service or person with something worse.

Sometimes you're afraid to hurt someone's feelings, or feel obligated, telling yourself that a contract is a contract and you have to live with it.

In the final analysis, a bad deal is a bad deal and an impaired relationship may not be mendable.

The sooner you can honestly face it—hopefully with diplomacy—and either negotiate a settlement or walk away from a bad situation the sooner you'll be blessed.

UNSHACKLING FROM DISORDER

Who doesn't get confused when he can't find something. *Where the heck did I write down that phone number?*

Who doesn't get agitated when she can't find her car keys. *Who moved the keys; they belong right here!*

Who doesn't kick themselves, over and over, when an opportunity is missed, because it slipped their mind? *Why didn't I write that down?*

Disorder is a form of imprisonment. And most of the time the only way for you to "get out of jail free" is to change something in your own life. Disorder is usually not someone else's fault. It's yours. Oh, I know, the kids can create a mess. Your spouse loses things. And others may be to blame to some degree. But by and large—admit it—disorder is something we *allow* to happen.

How do you get rid of it? Make it a top priority to change the way you think and act; then begin to influence those around you through your changed behavior.

As a television executive, I used to be late for meetings constantly. I thought nothing of it. Then one day my great-aunt said something about her Bible-study meetings that altered my attitude and the way I subsequently acted.

She said, "I always like to get to my meetings on time. Otherwise it would say that I consider my time more important than my friends' time."

That simple sentence—not even intended as a direct communication to judge me—struck home. I thought about all those producers and TV studio executives that I'd kept waiting for meetings simply because my rank allowed me to do it.

Weren't they busy people too?

Yet, the message I was silently communicating to them was: *I'm more important than you are.*

I changed. I replaced the disorder of tardiness with the order of timeliness.

Not only did I begin setting an example that my staff could

emulate by arranging my schedule so that I could be on time, but I elevated the priority of returning phone calls in a timely fashion as well.

Funny, I can still hear my great-aunt's sweet voice: "Otherwise it would say that I consider my time more important than my friends' time."

UNSHACKLING FROM FEAR AND ANXIETY— CARLA

Carla, whom you met earlier, tells another story about a time when she was shackled by worry about an illness she'd been suffering from for many months. Constantly demons were challenging her faith.

To try to get a handle on these matters, she decided to take a stress management course.

One evening the teacher commenced a dialogue about the importance of maintaining a good mental attitude and the power of positive thinking. Then she added, "I don't mean acting like Pollyanna."

Carla had not heard that reference before.

"Who is Pollyanna?" she asked the teacher.

"'Pollyanna was a storybook girl who suffered great tragedy yet always looked at the bright side of things,'" Carla quoted her teacher as saying, not fully understanding why such a positive attitude would not be admirable.

Later on, Carla read a summary of the story:

Pollyanna's philosophy of life centers on what she calls "The Glad Game," an optimistic attitude she learned from her father. The game consists of finding something to be glad about in every situation. It originated in an incident one Christmas when Pollyanna, who was hoping for a doll in the missionary barrel, found only a pair of crutches inside. Making the game up on the spot, Pollyanna's father taught her to look at the good side of things—in this case, to be glad about the crutches because "We don't need 'em!"[27]

The next day Carla and her daughter were shopping at a thrift store.

"My daughter came up to me with a book that she wanted to buy," says Carla, "and I couldn't believe my eyes. It was *Pollyanna!*"

Because of the power of the godwink, Carla took the book into her hands and opened it like a rare volume. Something fell out.

"Look, Mom," said her daughter, stooping to pick up what had fallen to the floor. "This part of the book is for you."

She handed Carla a little prayer card with a picture of Jesus.

"His arms were outstretched and He seemed to be looking straight at me," Carla remembers.

She felt an inexplicable peace.

"It was just too uncanny. There are some things that just go beyond coincidence," says Carla, shaking her head. "Every night I read the prayers on that card. My illness has not gone away, but I have a renewed strength to face whatever challenges may lie ahead."

Pollyanna helped Carla unshackle herself from her fears. Perhaps you can try the same "Glad Game" with the demons that challenge your faith from time to time. Perhaps you'll also be glad for crutches you don't need.

FEEL THE FREEDOM

Like Tyler Perry, Carla Cooper, and Anne Beiler, you can feel enormous liberty when you unshackle yourself from the unforgiveness that is holding you back, preventing God from showering you with blessings.

You will be astonished—as they were—by the freedom of becoming unshackled from resentment. You'll move into a harmonious flow with God's purpose for your life, confident that you now know what you need to do, in order to get where you want to go.

Perhaps you can see yourself becoming a storybook character—the Little Boat That Should—when you cut yourself loose from all things holding you at the dock of life: debt, bad deals, bad habits, disorder, and fear. You can feel God putting the wind beneath your sails as you move ahead, toward your destiny, encountering the people and events He has Divinely Aligned along your way.

GPS STEP 4

UNSHACKLE YOUR BAGGAGE

Learn to unshackle yourself from hurtful habits, resentments, and guilt, cutting yourself free to allow God to propel you more quickly to your destination.

STEP OUT IN FAITH AND BELIEVE YOU'LL ARRIVE

How many times have you heard yourself say, "If I hadn't met so-and-so, at that very time and place, I would never have ended up with the career I pursued, or the love of my life," or something else you value highly?

When you've experienced an "accidental encounter" with someone who led you onto a whole new path in your life, you, at the time, most likely did not consider it Divine Alignment, nor that a godwink was involved.

Yet it is a salient purpose of this book to raise your consciousness to the number of times you are divinely aligned with just the right person, at just the right time, through events that may seem coincidental, but when you consider the monumental odds, you have no other word but *godwinks* to express it.

Further, I have a thesis that Divine Alignment, as well as godwinks, occur with greater frequency when you are actively involved in tasks that you believe God wants you to be doing: when you are stepping out in faith heading for what you believe to be your destiny.

What do I mean by "stepping out in faith"?

I mean that you are getting up from the baggage you may be sitting on alongside your highway in life, leaving the baggage behind, and striking out, fully trusting that your Navigator is beckoning you, and that you are encased in the armor of faith, heading toward your destination.

Wise words in the ancient scriptures support this notion:

I've got my eye on the goal,
where God is beckoning us onward.

PHILIPPIANS 3:14 (THE MESSAGE)

Let's see how this thesis of stepping out in faith unfolds in the life of a young boy in an African village where genocide—the mass killing of an entire segment of the population—is all around him, where poverty is the only way of life, and where *hope* is a seemingly unattainable four-letter word.

DUSTY ROADS AND DREAMS

Emmanuel was a boy of ten.

"Daddeeeee . . . you said we'd be safe," he wailed in agony.

The most shocking images of his short life had just been indelibly imprinted on Emmanuel Mutangana's mind. Images of the mutilated body of his beloved father would, for years, foster anger and resentment against the Rwandan murderers who crossed into the presumably safe haven of Uganda to hunt down his father.

"My mother shielded me from the gruesome details, but I begged my father's friend to tell me; I needed to pursue the ones who murdered my dad," remembers Emmanuel. "I was full of misery. I didn't cry. I couldn't feel happiness."

"My father had been a wonderful provider. He was kind and generous," says Emmanuel, and then his mother's health began to fail and she lived only a few years longer.

He describes a subsequent life of living on the streets and caring for his siblings. There were many nights that he would simply knock on a door and say, "Can we have food and stay here? We have no place to sleep."

With the help of an organization called World Vision, Emmanuel was able to enroll in a missionary school where an American man from North Carolina, Charles Evans, became a critical bridge for him.

"He told me that only Jesus could mend my hurting heart and take away the dark, angry thoughts that I was carrying with me."

Watch how Emmanuel's encounter with Charles Evans—a Divine Alignment—became a critical turn of the rudder in his young life.

"Come watch some music videos," invited Charles one day.

Emmanuel was captivated. A woman in the video sang unlike anything he had ever heard—her soaring voice and the music lifted him up, made him feel at peace, safer. Her name was Sandi Patty.

"There is strength in the name of the Lord, there is power in the name of the Lord, there is hope in the name of the Lord," sang Sandi, to an audience of thousands of people, on the tape.

He was mesmerized, watching her move across the platform against a backdrop with star like streaks, causing him to wonder, *Is that what heaven itself looks like?*

Aided by World Vision, Emmanuel learned to read music and sing. He was taught to play an old piano, the only one in the Ugandan village. Long in need of repair, with broken strings, it was available only after midnight for Emmanuel to practice on.

He was drawn to music. He found that singing the words of spiritual songs—especially Sandi Patty's—were God's tools to soothe his hurting heart. Verses like "How does a sparrow fly in a boundless sky? It's a miracle!" were like prayers, pulling him closer to God. And the closer he felt, the more distant were his feelings of anger and resentment.

Reading the Bible also became a soothing antidote for his anguish. He recalls reading "Bear a little longer with me."

"It felt like a neighbor sending me a note," says Emmanuel, who was feeling the emotional propulsion that comes from stepping out in faith.

By the time he was twenty-one, the era of horrific genocide ended and he was able to return to his native Rwanda. As his musical talents improved, he was invited to sing and play at churches.

"One evening a woman walking by heard me singing in English through the open door of a church," says Emmanuel. "She enjoyed my music and wanted to introduce me to an American couple."

Another critical Divine Alignment for Emmanuel. Note how this encounter will reverberate for years to come.

"George and Betty Jackson were veterinarians from the USA—Tennessee—who said they'd come to Rwanda to help people like me," said Emmanuel, "and soon they were telling me about a Bible college called Daystar, and if I liked, they could help me go there."

Weeks before Emmanuel left for his first semester, George said, "Emmanuel, you need to learn table manners. You may be invited to dine in the company of important people and you'll need to know how to properly use a knife and fork, and how to eat soup with a spoon."

He and Betty taught him.

In a stream of godwinks, not more than one week later, Emmanuel was invited to dine at the home of the president of Rwanda. The president's wife had learned of his singing and asked if he could spend a few days teaching her children how to sing and play the piano. Soup was served for lunch. And he knew how to eat it properly.

In retrospect, meeting George and Betty Jackson was a

life-changing Divine Alignment for Emmanuel. He often wondered, *What would my life have become if the door to that church had been closed that evening. Instead, it "happened" to be open.*

"God has a purpose for me," he concluded, "and God has influenced George and Betty as well as others like Charles Evans to help move me in the direction He has planned for me."

Emmanuel began to observe that good things seemed to happen to people who, bolstered by their faith, were willing to step *out* in faith, and were willing to step *up* to introduce themselves to people, placing themselves where they could be visible to others. He discovered, over and over, that whenever he practiced that notion, Divine Alignment almost certainly followed.

George and Betty remained a direction finder for Emmanuel. They talked to him about going to America to study at a Bible college in Minnesota. Again they offered to pay his way.

After a few years of study, Emmanuel was drawn to Georgetown University near Washington, D.C. There, his college roommate became a Godwink Link—the unwitting messenger of a godwink—to a multi-national event resulting in a speaking invitation for him.

"As compensation they told me I could name a charity to receive a donation," said Emmanuel. "I immediately said, 'World Vision—in Rwanda I saw how thousands of children were helped by World Vision.'"

This simple compensation for Emmanuel's services—an opportunity to have a small donation made in his name to an organization that had impacted his childhood—was another critical Divine Alignment.

Several weeks later he received a call from a lady who identified herself as a leader at World Vision. She thanked him for the charitable contribution and invited him to come to New York to speak at an event. That experience was repeated several more times, with audiences always drawn to Emmanuel's story of a young boy whose family had been devastated by Rwandan genocide, but who had been divinely guided to where he was at that moment.

"One day the World Vision woman called me and said she'd like me to travel to Dallas to meet with some women who were part of a ministry that supported World Vision," said Emmanuel. "So, of course, I said yes."

Seated at the table in Dallas with several charming ladies identified as speakers for an organization called Women of Faith, Emmanuel learned that they performed at huge arenas across the country to audiences of ten to fifteen thousand people, thirty times a year.

Mary Graham, president of Women of Faith, led the conversation, introducing the others, including a spunky grandmother with spiked hair and colorful tennis shoes named Patsy Claremont.

"Tell us your story, Emmanuel," invited Mary.

In five minutes he told how, at age ten, he'd learned of his father's murder, his subsequent period of anger and depression, and, after losing his mother, how he cared for his siblings.

"World Vision was a lifeline for me," he told Mary and the others.

Reflected in the faces of every woman around the table was the enormous compassion they felt for Emmanuel's journey. And they all seemed pleased when he told them that he had taught children to play music, and that music was very important to him.

"What singer do you like the most?" asked Patsy.

"A lady named Sandi Patty," said Emmanuel without hesitation. "More than anything else, a videotape of Sandi Patty lifted me from anger and darkness." With a gleaming smile, he added, "I *love* Sandi Patty."

Eyes visibly widened as the women at the table quickly glanced at each other and smiled.

"Have you ever met Sandi Patty?" asked Mary Graham, almost coyly.

"Oh *no*," said Emmanuel, responding like someone who'd been asked if they had ever met the Queen of England or the president.

"Would you like to?" continued Mary, with a broad smile, pausing a beat, then adding, "She performs with us."

Emmanuel was stunned.

"I have her phone number," said Patsy, starting to dial her cell phone.

Sandi Patty remembers receiving the phone call like it happened yesterday.

"Patsy was talking excitedly. She said, 'Sandi, you have to hear this story!'

"Soon Mary was on the speakerphone introducing me to a young man named Emmanuel. Then it became all quiet. I thought we'd lost the connection, until I realized it was a very emotional moment."

Mary Graham allowed Emmanuel to gather himself, then prompted the conversation by asking, "Emmanuel, what is your favorite Sandi Patty song?"

With a still-wavering voice, he replied indirectly.

"When I was a boy with no home or parents, I walked the dusty roads of Africa; in my pocket I carried my only possession—a sheet of music for 'In the Name of the Lord.'" He glanced at the others, adding, "*That* is my favorite song."

"That's one of my favorite songs too," said Sandi softly, over the phone.

"Would you sing it for me, Sandi?" asked Emmanuel, his voice now matching his lustrous smile.

"Only if you sing it with me," Sandi replied with a laugh.

She began.

"Over the phone, music and God collapsed the distance between us," remembers Sandi.

Tears streamed from the eyes of everyone around the table, all realizing that they were not only witnessing a special moment in time, but that they were part of it.

"There is strength in the Name of the Lord," sang Sandi.

"There is hope in the name of the Lord." Emmanuel's voice blended with hers.

"Blessed is He who comes, in the name of the Lord," they finished in strong unison.

"When I returned to my room that afternoon, I lay on my bed and wept," says Emmanuel. "I said, 'God, you are amazing! Look how you have taken a ten-year-old boy out of a place of death and darkness and brought me to this place of joy in my life.'"

Again and again he replayed the unbelievable events in his mind.

And he was especially excited about Mary Graham's invitation; she said Women of Faith would soon be performing in Washington, D.C., at a huge arena. She asked if he'd like to come and sit with them, and hear Sandi Patty sing in person.

Wow, he thought.

Sandi Patty was astonished at how a surprise phone conversation with a boy from Africa had affected her.

"Never did I dream that the music I have been so blessed to sing over the years could play such an integral part in the life of one of the World Vision kids," she said, revisiting her memory of the call with Emmanuel.

"I began putting together the pieces of the time frame; when Emmanuel was a young teenager, so drawn to my music, giving him light, it was the very season when things were very tough in my own life."

She began to see that by God's wondrous ways, the global connection between two anguished people, six thousand miles apart, was a single piece of music—"In the Name of the Lord."

"That very song was so often my prayer onstage," she says.

"The second verse is, 'When my plans have fallen through, and when my strength is nearly gone, when there's nothing left to do, but just depend on you, and the power of your name.' I would sing it with extra conviction because I needed it so desperately in my life."

Three months after the phone call Sandi had another surprise. On the Women of Faith shuttle bus that was transporting the cast from their Washington, D.C., hotel to the arena, Mary Graham leaned back and said, "Sandi, I forgot to tell you; you're going to meet Emmanuel today. Remember? The young man from Africa you spoke with by phone?"

"He's here? He's here?" Sandi asked excitedly.

Butterflies filled her stomach along with a feeling of excitement.

"When I saw him backstage, we hugged for a long time," says Sandi.

With tears emerging in their eyes, Emmanuel addressed Sandi with an African term of endearment.

"Auntie, look what I have!"

He pulled a paper from his pocket.

"This is your song. My only possession, that I carried with me . . ."

". . . on the dusty roads of Africa," finished Sandi.

They smiled, gazed at each other, and hugged once more.

But, for now, there was no time to linger—it was show time.

In a section reserved for special guests, Emmanuel sat like a wide-eyed schoolboy. His heart raced as his eyes looked all around the huge arena, his mind absorbing the cacophony of fifteen thousand excited women, filling the air with cheers as each speaker and singer stepped onto the Women of Faith stage in the round. From where he sat he could see his heroine, Sandi Patty, no more than forty feet away, seated with other speakers and performers.

Then he watched as Mary Graham climbed the steps to center

stage, and listened as her voice filled the arena with a slight echo. Pictures of smiling African children appeared on the screen as Mary told how World Vision is an island of hope for so many children who have no food, shoes, or shelter.

Then he heard his own name as Mary briefly told his story, testimony for what World Vision was able to do to help a single boy and his siblings.

Then he heard her say, "Would you like to meet him?"

He had a momentary impulse to cover his ears as the audience cheered so loudly. Instead, he was on his feet, bounding up the steps, and stepping up in faith, into the very scene he'd remembered as a ten-year-old—from the Sandi Patty video—with the star-filtered spotlights in the distance that made him wonder if he was seeing heaven itself.

As Mary told the audience about the phone call three months earlier during which he and Sandi had, Emmanuel was almost speechless.

"When Mary interviewed Emmanuel onstage," says Sandi, "I honestly didn't know she was going to call me up onstage as well. But—it was so the right thing to do."

Again the roar of the crowd was thunderous as she climbed the steps.

"And when Mary said, 'Do something together,' Emmanuel and I both realized that the *only* song we could do together was 'In the Name of the Lord.'"

Sandi began to sing a cappella and Emmanuel quickly joined into this impromptu duet.

There is strength in the name of the Lord
There is power in the name of the Lord
There is hope in the name of the Lord
Blessed is he who comes in the name of the Lord

For the next three minutes every one of us in the arena felt the joy of witnessing a boy's dream come true. Yes, I said "us"—through a marvelous godwink, my wonderful wife, Louise, was a speaker for Women of Faith that year, and we were openmouthed and overjoyed as Emmanuel joined Sandi in singing the song that was so special in each of their lives, "In the Name of the Lord."

Sandi summarizes her feelings about that storybook day, remembering how, a decade before, she and Emmanuel were two people who'd never met, yet whose lives were invisibly connected by a single piece of music.

"The *truth* of God's word ministered to two people in two very different circumstances. It ministered to Emmanuel on the dusty roads of Africa, and it ministered to me as I sang it on the dusty roads of my own personal life."

What are the odds of this story ever unfolding? With God and His Divine Alignment, there are no odds. But, aren't we glad that Emmanuel stepped out in faith so we could experience the joy of this story?

IF GOD IS GOD, WHY CAN'T HE JUST MOVE ME?

Is this a question we've all asked: "If God wants me to arrive at a particular destiny, why doesn't He just pick me up and move me there?"

I've concluded that if God wanted perfect little robots to do exactly what He wants, when He wants, He would have made us that way.

He didn't.

He gave us minds, bodies, and all the tools to get through life in order to propel ourselves, under our own free will, to the destiny He has prescribed for us. He wants us to walk on our own, *beside* Him, becoming self-sufficient and independent, not having to carry us from one place to the next like a stubborn child who refuses to walk. That's why He has given us free will.

With built-in free will we are free to stumble, to make mistakes, be inappropriate, and even do stupid, dangerous things. When we misstep and fall, He'll help us up and teach us at the same time.

As a parent, when your child falls and lets out a cry, you use your experience to teach her how to walk taller, steadier, and with greater confidence.

"Our sword cannot be sharpened by butter. It must be ground against stone."

God knows that the valleys you face in life are hard and scary. But He also knows that the stress of tragedy is like the stress of pumping iron to build muscle; it's all a part of His plan to make us stronger, better. Our sword cannot be sharpened by butter. It must be ground against stone.

Sometimes, to stay on task, heading for what we believe is our destiny, we need to keep on stepping out in faith—believing that Divine Alignment will unfold.

DRIVING INTO THE FIRE

The radio newsman had a higher pitch to his voice as he told how the fires were raging out of control in Southern California, engulfing homes and endangering lives. Many highways were shut down, he reported.

Os Hillman was worried. Gauging the traffic against time, in his northward quest, a four-hour drive to a speaking engagement, he now needed to add another factor, his safety. Through the windshield he could see an ominous curtain of black smoke hanging right over the skyline he was heading for.

Halfway into his journey he spotted a gas station and made a quick decision to pull in, gas up, and assess the conditions ahead.

"The interstate's closed north of here," said the lady at the pump next to him. "If you're going that way, you might not get back."[1]

What do I do? Call and cancel my commitment? thought Os. He hated that notion; canceling commitments was not in his repertoire.

Fear began to seize him as he thought about being stranded in a strange place. He spoke to the Navigator. *Lord, is this a warning for me to turn back? Or is this the enemy attempting to block my path?*

He went into the store to purchase a map. Divine Alignment was about to occur.

As Os was poring over a map, a man walked up to him.

"Where you trying to get to?" the man asked.

Os told him.

"Well, the interstate's open north of the fires, and it just so happens that's where I'm going. You'll have to follow me," stated the man, with a tone of confidence.

For the next several miles Os "stepped out in faith" by following the man's truck through very unfamiliar areas on all sorts of side roads.

Finally they emerged next to an on-ramp for the interstate, and the billowing smoke was now south of them. The man waved to Os. He signaled enormous appreciation in return, and continued his journey, now having the peace of mind that he would get to his speaking engagement on time, and safely.

I could never have gotten here myself, thought Os as he drove. *Thank You, God.*[2]

He then assessed what had happened to him, with amazement; how, just before he walked into the convenience store, he had prayed for reassurance that he was doing the right thing by stepping out in faith, and continuing his mission. And, within seconds, a man was standing next to him, like an angelic messenger, delivering both the reassurance and the guidance.

What caused that man to be there at that moment? Divine Alignment.

What caused Os to encounter him? He took a step—he spoke up—he asked directions.

Persevere so that when you have done the will of God,
you will receive what He has promised you.

HEB 10:36–37 (NIV)

AS YOU STEP OUT, BELIEVE IN THE OUTCOME

When you muster the will to lift yourself up from that baggage beside the road, do it with confidence; step out in faith, *believing* that you will indeed be arriving at the outcome and the destination you are seeking. Be certain that there will be godwinks as signposts all along your path. And that you'll be divinely aligned with others who will help you along.

See it.

See yourself pleased by your arrival at your destination.

The man in the next story, in a most harrowing situation, didn't just *believe*, he said, "We *knew* our prayer was going to be answered."

THE BELIEVING TRUCKERS

The image of fifty seasoned truck drivers, some with leathered skin, some with beards, did not fit the stereotype of tough-as-nails truckers. They were standing in a circle, praying.

A driver like Ron Lancz, sixty-two, would be expected to be "spittin' tobacca" from a face scarred by barroom brawls. But Ron and this group of truckers made it their practice to stay in contact with "Someone up there, bigger than all of us," and on this day they were very concerned.

For three weeks the population around the nation's capital had been frozen in fear. Terrorists known as the Beltway Snipers had already killed ten and wounded three—mothers in parking lots and fathers driving home from work. Every man, woman, and child looked over their shoulders as they went about their daily tasks, wondering, *Who will be next to be caught in the killer's crosshairs?*

When Ron and his fellow truckers decided to put on the protective armor of the Almighty by communicating their concerns to Him, something happened.

"We knew our prayer was going to be answered," said Ron firmly. "That's the way we believe."

Four days later Ron was on Highway 70, fifty miles to the north of D.C. It was 1 a.m. He was tired. Just five more hauls and he'd be hanging it up for good: retirement.

Should I stop and catch a half hour of shut-eye? he asked himself.

Auspiciously, he came upon a rest stop and slowed his twelve-wheeler rig to pull in.

That radio report he'd heard a few minutes earlier was still on his mind. An APB—all points bulletin—for a blue or burgundy 1990 Chevrolet Caprice. "Use extreme caution, the Beltway Snipers are armed and dangerous," said the stern-voiced newsman.

As Ron turned the wheel to pass a darkened car in the rest stop, he leaned forward, squinted, and brought his truck to a crawl to examine it. That was it! A burgundy Chevy Caprice. About 1990.

The adrenaline rushed through him.

Quick. Make a decision. What to do? Then he had an idea.

He kept his giant rig crawling to the end of the rest stop. Came to a halt. Backed up and then pulled forward to block the exit.

He called 911 and reported the suspicious car.

Then he radioed another trucker, who, it turned out, was only a mile or so away. Quickly, breathlessly, Ron instructed him to pull into the entrance of the rest stop, blocking it from that end.

Then he waited. In the dark. He noticed his own heavy breathing as the minutes ticked by, continually shifting his eyes to the dark car, suspecting that inside were armed and dangerous men who had no reason not to jump out, guns blazing, to kill him!

As the waiting grew long, he took advantage of the opportunity to again speak with his Navigator. Asking for protection. And for the swift arrival of the police.

Suddenly Ron was enveloped in a sea of flashing blue and red lights. The suspect's car was rapidly surrounded, and the occupants, homegrown terrorists John Allen Muhammad and John Lee Malvo, were ordered out and taken away.

With a sigh, Ron said, "Thank God."

Ron Lancz had firmly held to his *belief* that the prayers that he and the other truckers had uttered *would* be answered. And, until that moment in time, he was an ordinary man with an ordinary life. Yet he was suddenly called upon to play an extraordinary role on life's stage, and he didn't know he'd have a starring role in the final scene.

WHAT HAVE WE LEARNED?

Emmanuel Mutangana, a boy growing up in Africa, stepped out in faith, believing that God was directing his path, and in a mind-blowing outcome, he was transported to the very stage in America that he once imagined was heaven, and found himself singing with the very lady who inspired him. Os Hillman, fearful of a raging California fire, stepped out in faith to complete a speaking obligation. Along the way a man—perhaps a Divinely Aligned angel—offered to guide him safely past the fire to be on time for his appointment. And Ron Lancz, the trucker who believed that his communications with the Navigator—through prayer—would indeed rescue the populace of the nation's capital from the Beltway Snipers, stepped out in faith, never thinking that God was going to use him in such a pivotal way. They all had faith. They all arrived at the destinations of their desire.

THE PRINCIPLE OF BELIEVING

For prayer to work in your life, it's essential for you to *believe* it's working, to believe it *will* be answered in one of three ways: **yes**, **no**, or **not right now**. God hears every prayer.

Often He will say **yes** right away and you'll know it.

If His answer is **no**, you might not find out why till much later on, when you have a better perspective.

If the answer is **not right now**, it often means that God has to put other people and events into proper positioning for your prayer to be answered. By Divinely Aligning you with others along your path, God will provide you with something much better than you ever imagined.

> *God hears every prayer . . . His answer is . . . yes, no, or not right now.*

BUT . . . WHAT HAPPENS WHEN MY PRAYER IS *NOT* ANSWERED?

There are people of great faith, Norman Vincent Peale, Abraham Lincoln, and Mother Teresa among them, who, at one time or another, doubted their faith when they felt that their prayers went unanswered.

Really?

Absolutely true.

When you find yourself in a similar situation, try asking yourself these three questions:

- Am I Sure My Prayer Hasn't Already Been Answered?

Prayers are seldom answered exactly the way we expect them to be. In fact, we're often surprised with *how* they get answered. You may even find yourself saying, "Only God could have answered my prayer that way, perhaps to confirm that it could have come only from Him!" So rethink your situation and be certain your prayer wasn't answered when you weren't paying attention.

- Have I Given God Enough Time to Answer My Prayer?

Have I given Him plenty of time, like several weeks, months, or years? For God to realign the thinking and actions of the many people along your path, it may take considerable time for your Divine Alignments to unfold.

- Is There Something I Need to Be Doing, Myself, to Unlock God's Blessings?

Harken back to the last chapter on unshackling baggage and examine the things you may need to do—resentments you need to release, debts you need to retire, or things you need to put into order—that will pull up the anchors you have on your own life, thereby allowing God to present you with the supernatural outcome of your prayer. Then, step out in faith.

GPS STEP 5

STEP OUT IN FAITH AND BELIEVE YOU'LL ARRIVE

Your destiny will not come to you. You need to continually talk with the Navigator, programming your GPS, then step out in faith. Your highway to Providence will continue to unfold, even on the most uncertain days, regardless of the twists and turns you encounter.

READ THE SIGNS, RECALCULATE, AND ACCELERATE

Up to this point most of our discussion has been centered on getting ready to cast off on your life's journey: setting your GPS; discovering your inner compass; creating a map; unshackling yourself from your baggage; and building faith to believe that you'll indeed arrive at your destination.

Now you're on the highway.

How do you know if you're heading in the right direction? Going too fast? Too slow? Or whether the road is Slippery When Wet?

Read the signs.

Surely, sometimes the signs will come to you directly from your inner compass. The "still, small voice within" will speak to you, providing an instinctive message that you missed your turn, are on the wrong path, or heading in the wrong direction.

Additional signposts for you, providing you allow yourself to see them, will be godwinks, the messages from above that pop up like little coincidences all along your way. They're messages of reassurance that you're never alone, that your Navigator has you on his GPS.

In case the meaning of *godwink* is not yet clear, this is my dictionary definition:

godwink [gawd•wingk] (n)

1. An event or experience, often identified as coincidence, so astonishing it could have come only from a divine source.

2. A word that fills the vacancy in the English language for *answered prayer*.

WHEN WE'RE UNSURE OF OURSELVES

The good thing about signposts is that they help us feel more certain during periods of uncertainty.

Have you ever driven in a storm—snow, rain, or dust—where your visibility was barely past the hood ornament? You grip the wheel, lean forward, gaze into the blankness, with pupils that may be dilated like marbles. You worry that someone up ahead will stop quickly and you'll ram into *them*. Strangely, that's the same motivation for you, almost insanely, to keep on driving when you can't see a thing; you're afraid someone will pile into *your* rear end.

Then, like a gift from the heavens—a sign telling you that you're parallel with a rest stop or a gas station—you're able to pull over, out of harm's way, and breathe normally again.

"Godwinks . . . Godwinks are those kinds of signs in your life. They help bring certainty to uncertain situations.

bring certainty to I'm fond of this simile: godwinks are like the *uncertain situations."* wink you received as a kid from Grandma—a quiet, comforting communication that said, "Hey, kid, I'm thinking of you right now." Imagine your father saying, "Hey, kid, you're not alone, everything is going to be okay."

SIGNPOSTS OF GRADUATION

There is no real preparation for losing someone you love.

No schools to attend.

No homework to do.

Losing a parent is a passage most of us go through with great difficulty, twice in a lifetime.

Michelle Krouyer was devastated when her mother, Shirley Williams, died of breast cancer. Even though she could tell herself that her mother was now in a better place, she was immobilized by grief.

"I was unable to return to work as a nurse," she says. "I sat on my sofa crying all day."

A month passed and she was still struggling with the agony of loss when she heard that one her coworkers at the hospital, Alma, had lost a child; her twenty-four-year-old daughter had died suddenly, unexpectedly. Michelle felt terrible.

"It's one thing to lose your mother who has lived a full life, but can you imagine losing a child who had a whole lifetime ahead of her?" she says.

A nagging feeling inside beckoned Michelle to go to the funeral. She argued with herself. It was an hour away. She was frightened that it was in a section of New Orleans she'd never been to. Still— the tugging was persuasive.

Michelle put on a black dress and began the trek, all the while thinking what an awful burden Alma and her family had to endure versus her own.

But, when she arrived at the church, she was surprised. It wasn't draped in black. In fact, she was the only person dressed in black. Everyone else wore white or colorful outfits. They were joyful. Especially Alma.

"Don't you feel sorry for my daughter or your mama," Alma told Michelle brightly as she greeted her. "They are both rejoicing with the Lord. *We* are the ones suffering down here."

As Michelle sat in the pew, soaking in the uplifting ambience, she compared it with her own mourning; here *they* were, celebrating this young woman's graduation into heaven, while *she* had become immobilized—unable to function.

Bright rays of sunlight streaked through the stained-glass windows as Michelle looked upward, feeling oddly envious.

Why am I feeling sad while they are so joyful? she silently asked God.

At that very moment there was a godwink. The scent of the same perfume her mother, Shirley Williams, used to wear wafted past her. It was clearly distinct. No mistaking it.

Michelle was puzzled. She glanced down at the funeral program she held in her hand.

She was jolted. Her eyes had fallen upon the name of her mother. Shirley Williams!

How could this be?!

A moment later she understood. It was a second godwink. The program stated that Alma's daughter was preceded in death by her grandmother—whose name was also Shirley Williams.

"I suddenly felt a peace come over me," whispered Michelle. "As I inhaled the scent of her perfume, in the warm rays of sun through the stained-glass windows, it was as if my mom's arms were around me."

She also felt an instant comprehension of why she had been so compelled to travel the distance to be at that exact place where Divine Alignment would unfold, at that very moment. God wanted her to realize that her mother, and Alma's daughter, had both simply graduated.

At graduations, the graduate is never sad. It's the rest of us—we who are left behind—who feel sadness.

As she left the church, Michelle smiled to herself, now confident that her mother was in a place from where—given the choice—she would choose not to return.

• • •

As I've said, we all graduate. Some sooner than the rest. But, when you lose someone you love, try to remember Michelle's experience. Look for the signposts of comfort that God will be sending you—the godwinks of reassurance: "Hey kid, everything will be all right."

WHAT IF THERE ARE NO SIGNS ALONG MY PATHS?

This may be a question stalking you. "What if I've taken all the steps laid out in this book—I get out there on my highway, heading for the destination I've mapped for myself—and there are NO SIGNS. What then?"

I ask you, have you ever been on a road where there are absolutely no signs whatsoever?

Even on back roads in most states, there are small signs every so often, identifying where you are. In the absence of that, there are the signs we recognize by the way the sun is heading . . . up in the east and down in the west. You can even look at the Big Dipper in the night skies and know you're heading north.

Complete isolation from signage is very rare.

Same with signs from above. The most common reason why godwink signs are not seen by people is this: we have decided to switch off our acceptance of them; our brain has told us that it's impossible for them to be there, so we don't see them.

The more you see godwinks, the more you see them.

The opposite is also true. As on any highway, when you consciously look for signs, you see many more than you thought were there. And godwink aficionados will tell you: the more you see godwinks, the more you see them.

BIKES, MIKES, AND SIGNS

Barb and Kermit Gephart climbed onto their three-wheeled motor-cycle to make the day's journey from Gatlinburg, Tennessee, along the breathtakingly beautiful Blue Ridge Parkway, to Cherokee, North Carolina. This stretch of "America's Favorite Drive" is a ribbon of road, dizzily winding along the high ridges of the Appalachian Mountains. The two-lane, limited-access roadway unfolds in a pristine panorama devoid of commercial signage.

"We'd not seen a ranger all day, and there was little off-season traffic," says Barb, explaining that the twists and turns of the roadway tended to self-regulate vehicles from exceeding the forty-five-mile-an-hour speed limit.

"This is also a stretch of the parkway where there are no berms or shoulders; except for an occasional scenic overlook, there's no place to pull over," adds Kermit.

Barb brought the story to its point: "It was the end of the day, and we were nearly ten miles from Cherokee, when we suddenly had a flat tire."

They quickly considered the severity of their situation:

"The rear tire was flat, and there are no spares on a cycle," says Kermit.

Barbara continues: "With no shoulders, no place to pull over—literally on the edge of a mountain—sitting there on the road, waiting for someone to help, would be inviting a collision."

"There was no cell-phone service in the mountains," says Kermit. "No rangers, no people to turn to for help, and it was getting dark. Even if someone *could* stop, one of us would have to leave the other to get to the next town, hope to find a tire dealer still open, or someone with a flatbed tow truck, to bring it back up the mountain to our Trike, sitting on the road, and load it up."

"All in all, it was a very frightening prospect," Barb concludes with a sigh.

With the tire now flapping, Kermit slowed the bike down as they rounded a curve. And there—right in front of them—was Divine Alignment of spectacular proportions! A signpost in the form of a fabulous godwink. Not only had they come upon an infrequent scenic pull-off, but there was a ranger, just getting into his car. They shouted and waved, getting his attention.

The ranger radioed his dispatcher to send a tow truck from Waynesville, about twenty-five miles away, and stayed with the couple for the next hour until they could be safely on their way.

"We learned the ranger's name was Mike, so I told him he was Michael 'our archangel,'" says Barb, still astonished by the extraordinary godwink of encountering him.

As they waited, another couple pulled into the scenic overlook and attempted, without avail, to see if a tire inflator might work.

"This man's name was also Mike," says Barb, smiling. "We thanked Mike for his efforts and waved them on their way."

Finally, the flatbed truck arrived, loaded them up, and they were on their way to Cherokee.

"As we drove down the mountain, we learned the driver's name. Another Mike." Barb gleamed.

Spending that night at a motel in Cherokee, Barb and Kermit, we can be sure, said their prayers, thanking God for His perfect care and timing.

"The next morning the only tire store in town installed the tire, and we were happily, blessedly, on our way," summarized Barb. "Oh, and by the way, the name of the tire man—can you believe it?—was Mike."

Barb and Kermit Gephart enjoyed their drive across the Blue Ridge Parkway; they *really* enjoyed it, fully appreciating that God was biking along with them, all the way. To have witnessed such precision in Divine Alignment—avoiding being stranded for the night, literally, on the side of a mountain was one thing, but sending a series of signposts in the form of godwinks . . . including four "arch-angels on earth" named Mike—was a clear confirmation from above.

"We knew God was taking care of us, but His endearing 'Mike-winks' will always be cemented into our minds," says Barb.

WHAT IF I GET LOST OR STUCK?

We all get lost sometimes. We take the wrong turn. Or we get stuck in a situation and don't know how to get out. Some would say, "That's what a GPS is for!"

True. And if you listen to the voice on your auto GPS, when you miss the turn or start going the wrong way, it will usually say, **"Re-calculate."**

We all must recalculate, all along our life's paths.

We sometimes need to backtrack a little, remaining in touch with, and listening to, the Navigator. Pray.

If you've lost your job with benefits, for example, you may not be able to find an equally good job right away . . . you may have to go back a bit . . . take a job with less pay and perks in a slightly different field, something that will let you reenter the workforce from a different on-ramp.

The first "recalculation" you probably need to make when that rug is pulled out from under you—when the news is not so gracefully delivered that you're being "downsized"—or whatever euphemism has been used to avoid the nasty-sounding word *fired*—is to realize that your world has not ended. In fact, you're a member of a huge club. Few people go through life without getting their walking papers. Maybe not as many times as Yogi Berra and Billy Martin got being axed in their baseball managing careers, but at least once or twice.

Bottom line, it hurts.

But it's not how you get knocked down that's important. It's how you get back up.

Talking to the Navigator, reassessing your strengths, and

recalculating the options should be at the top of your List of Things to Do.

In Chapter 4 I wrote about my own "downsizing" experience at ABC. As painful as it was, because it was the unjust outcome of a political maneuver, I never had the added embarrassment of having to read about it in the newspaper.

That was not the case with a fellow I've written about before. I imagine you've heard of him. Steve Jobs.

THE REINVENTION OF STEVE

At birth, Steve perceived he was rejected twice.

First, his mother rejected him by putting him up for adoption.

Second, the adoptive couple awaiting his arrival wanted a girl. So they rejected him too.

Despite this, everything turned out pretty well for Steve. A nice couple finally *did* adopt him, gave him a nice childhood, and by scrimping together every dime, saved enough to send their son to a small college.

Yet Steve wasn't what you'd call a social kid. Instead, he was the type who liked to figure out how things worked; he would take objects apart and put them back together again—just for the fun of it. What's more, Steve had no idea what he wanted to do in life.

Thus, college wasn't a comfortable fit. He couldn't comprehend why the courses on his required list—history, geography, philosophy—were necessary or how he'd apply what he learned in whatever career he decided to pursue.

So, after six months, he dropped out.

But what about his folks? He just couldn't let them down. So Steve remained at college . . . and dropped *in* on courses that were of interest to him.

For instance, he dropped in on a calligraphy course. For no

particular reason, learning about serif and sans serif typefaces and about the artistic subtlety of spaces between letters fascinated him.

But, by year's end, Steve got busted. His parents found out, and they made him return home.

When he did, Steve hung out with his old buddy, Woz. They started tinkering with a gadget—a computer—in the garage. They eventually called it an Apple.

Ten years later, at the ripe old age of thirty, Steven Jobs and Woz had gone from two guys tinkering in a garage to running a two-billion-dollar company. In his lap, he proudly held his brand-new Macintosh computer.[1]

And then . . . he got fired.

What?! How do you get fired from your own company?

He simply had a run-in with the board of directors, and this time he was rejected. Rejected big-time.

Steve was devastated. He later said he thought he had let down all entrepreneurs. He was about to run away from the Silicon Valley altogether. Then he thought, *Wait . . . I love what I do. I'm an inventor . . I just need to reinvent myself.*

Steve Jobs said later, "I didn't see it then, but it turned out that getting fired from Apple was the best thing that could have ever happened to me."

He repositioned his rejection and started over.

The heaviness of being successful, the inevitable demands that he top his last performance over and over again, "was replaced by the lightness of being a beginner again, less sure about everything. It freed me to enter one of the most creative periods of my life."

Steve set out to start a company he called NeXT, and its mission was to inaugurate a new technology. And a while later, with the pain of failure and rejection in his rearview mirror, Steve was led to another brainstorm. *Wouldn't it be great if we could use computers to generate an entire animated movie?*

So he bought out a small company called Pixar. He led the

development and production of the world's first fully animated movie using CGI—computer-generated imagery. The movie was called *Toy Story*.

As Steve Jobs focused on nurturing the growth of his two new companies, the firm he once founded was floundering. Apple was on the ropes. Wall Street gurus said the once-inventive computer manufacturer was washed up.

The board of directors at Apple determined they needed something new in order to survive. A new technology. The kind that Steve had developed at NeXT.

What sweet revenge! Apple came back to Jobs with their hats in their hands. They bought NeXT, and once again Steve Jobs was wandering the halls of Apple. That gave him the opportunity to make the board of directors another offer they couldn't refuse: hire him back as CEO for one dollar a year.

Apple did eventually pay Steve a better salary. And it happened just about the time he and his colleagues at Apple came up with the iPod—a technological development that altered how the world listens to music. The success of the iPod led to the iPhone and the iPad, on and on, and Apple was on its way to being a $350 billion company.

You can do the same thing Steve did with rejection: recalculate and reinvent yourself.

"None of this would have happened if I hadn't been fired," said Steve.

Nearly every one of us needs to recalculate our career pursuits at one time or another. If you aren't facing *forced* recalculation, as a result of the involuntary loss of your job, you may just wish to simply make a change. Or perhaps, like Steve Jobs, you'll reinvent yourself altogether. When you take any of these steps, step out in faith as we discussed in the last chapter, and expect Divine Alignment to occur.

For those of you who love to find the godwinks in my stories, you may wonder if there was one here. I shan't disappoint you.

When Steve Jobs was making his first Macintosh, he asked his engineers, "Instead of one typeface like the PCs have, what if we were to offer a whole array of fonts: serifs, sans serifs, and so on?"

That's right. The godwink of why all computers today have multiple fonts started when Steve Jobs dropped *in* on that calligraphy course years before.

You'll encounter many situations where you should expect Divine Alignment as you recalculate, including where you're going to live. Here's a story from one of my readers that exemplifies that point quite well.

THE SIGN IN THE BASEMENT

Sally and Jim were now ready.

After five years of marriage and having their fill of city dwelling, they were ready to return to Sally's hometown, buy a home, and start a family.

Of course their savings were meager. But, with the peace of mind that comes with knowing that they both had jobs lined up, they were cautiously confident they could swing it.

After several days of traipsing around town with a real estate broker, they were pooped and disheartened.

"Do you think there is *any* place here for us?" asked Sally forlornly. "I never thought houses would be so expensive in my own hometown."

"There *is* one more I can show you," said the broker, in measured fashion. "But . . . it's a real fixer-upper."

As Sally and Jim walked though the ramshackle Cape Cod–style cottage, occupied recently by an old man who was moved to a nursing home, they nearly choked on sour smells, tripping on decrepit debris.

Trying to bolster their optimism, the broker chimed, a bit too merrily, "Well, it *is* within your budget."

Sally and Jim looked at each other, panned their heads to survey the massive work ahead of them, sighed, and said, "Okay, we'll take it."

The next several months were back-breaking. Getting the place barely livable to move into, they came home from their nine-to-five jobs to rip down musty wallpaper, scrape off mildewy paint, roll up stained carpet, and cart more trash to the dump than anyone could imagine.

More than once they looked at each other with eyes that said, *Who are we kidding! This is not worth it.*

One Friday night, secretly wondering if their other partner, God, was pulling his load, Sally and Jim prayed for stamina and guidance. And a tangible sign.

"I hope this is not the sign," said Jim, holding the checkbook. "We're outta cash. We can't get the paint tomorrow."

"God, please speak to us," cried Sally in a tear-choked voice. "Give us some indication that we're doing the right thing. Let us know if this is our home."

Gently Jim placed his arm around her, squeezing her shoulders, signaling that he echoed her sentiments.

Letting out a breath, Jim said, "Well, instead of painting tomorrow, I'll do a dump run; all those dried-up paint cans in the basement."

The next morning Jim trod a path from the basement hatch doors to the trunk of his car. Each old paint can seemed heavier than the last. With each step he was asking the now-proverbial question, "Are we really meant to live here?"

As he lifted the last paint can sitting on yellowed newspapers that had lain on the basement floor for twenty-five years, according to the date on the masthead, he saw something that dropped his jaw.

"Sally!" he shouted up the cellar stairs. "Sally . . . come down here . . . you have to see this!"

Breathlessly, Sally padded down the steps with a quizzical look on her face. "What's the matter?"

"Look," said Jim, pointing to the old papers on the floor. "Look at that newspaper."

"Oh my God!" Sally exclaimed as she leaned over . . . and looked at *herself!*

It was a 1976 photograph on the front page of her hometown paper, with her maiden name printed underneath. She surveyed the newspapers, all stained with paint, faded through the years, except for the round circle where a paint can had protected her picture, almost as clear as new.

Sally and Jim embraced. They wept. It was the sign they'd asked for. God's personal sign to them: *Yes, this is home.*

Later, Sally said, "It was a godwink telling us that this house has always been ours . . . just waiting for us to come and make it new again!"

HOW DO I INTERPRET THE SIGNS?

How many times have you come up to a sign on a roadway that simply baffles you? Rather than clarifying the situation, it seems to make it more muddled. In a situation like this, I usually shake my head and grumble at an unseen, unknown Department of Highways bureaucrat.

> *"Signs are there to guide you, not to make decisions for you."*

Because we are constantly dealing with life situations that are not certain, questions consume us: "Will the guy like me?" "Will I get the job?" "Do I have the money to make it this month?" We desperately want concrete answers, such as "Marry the man" or "Yes, you have the job."

Here's the bottom line on signs: they are there to guide you, not to make decisions for you. All decisions, all choices, have to come from you in concert with that small, still voice within, our inner compass, God.

Even on the highway, the signs don't determine your destination. You do that. The signs are only there to let you know you're getting closer to where you want to go.

NOW GO. ACCELERATE

With everything in order, and the first six steps to program your God's Positioning System now under your belt, go. Put your foot on the accelerator. Cruise at speed limit. Your highway stretches before you, your destination is there for the taking.

GPS STEP 6

READ THE SIGNS, RECALCULATE, AND ACCELERATE

Godwinks are the reassuring signposts along your path let-ting you know you're going in the right direction. Watch for "danger" signs and recalculate from time to time by repro-gramming your GPS . . . God's Positioning System. Once on track, put your foot on the accelerator!

GRATEFULLY ARRIVE WITH A FULL WELL WITHIN

You probably had an Aunt Mae in your family—or someone like her.

My aunt Mae kept her living room furniture covered in plastic. She wanted to "keep it good for special occasions," such as a funeral. Same with the "good" china. The truth is, no one could ever remember sipping from the good china or sitting on anything but that stiff, uncomfortable plastic.

Aunt Mae suffered from a lack of personal peace. She was always "saving up for a rainy day" and would tell you, "When we make the big money, that's when we'll take a nice vacation."

Unfortunately Aunt Mae died before the rainy day or the big money ever came. But, for the first time in anyone's memory, the plastic came off the couch and the good china got used. At her own funeral.

I genuinely hope you'll arrive at that time and place in your life, long before Aunt Mae did, when you can honestly say, "I am *content* with myself! I have arrived. My life is filled with joy."

Too many of us are never at peace. We maintain our marathon struggles to be bigger, better, and have more. A bigger house. Better car. More stuff.

This is accompanied by a prevailing fear that if we don't maintain enough control over the people around us, the bubble will burst and we'll be left with nothing. No stuff.

That's not you, is it? Just a little?

If so, let's talk about how you can arrive at your destinations earlier . . . when you can truly say, "Yes! I *am* content. Regardless of how much money or how much stuff I have, I *am* filled with joy."

THE WONDERFUL WELL WITHIN

Each of us is born with a Well Within. It was made to store *contentment*. At birth, like the cellar of a new home, it's empty. Momentarily. For our desire is to fill it, as quickly and as often as possible. Day in and day out, we subconsciously try to fill the contentment void.

As infants, we cried out to satisfy the Well Within. Sometimes for food, but more often than not, simply to be held and hugged. The moment our parent picked us up, made silly faces and noises and rocked us, the Well Within was temporarily satiated with contentment.

As we grew, the unconscious quest to fill the Well Within expanded. In the absence of contentment we substituted other things: stuffing the space with food; pouring alcohol or drugs into the Well, or desperately trying to re-create the joy and contentment of being held in infancy by filling it with lustful activity.

For a few minutes or hours our minds may trick us into thinking that it's working. That we truly have found contentment. But it doesn't take long for the satisfaction to evaporate, for the Well to feel empty again.

We convince ourselves that: If I can just get rich and famous, my Well Within will always be overflowing with contentment.

But, honestly, does wealth and fame ever really fill the Well Within? The answer is always *no*.

As a nation, we spend billions every year trying to win lotteries. How many of those lottery winners whom we watched jumping for joy on the six o'clock news are now back in the poorhouse? Unfortunately, most of them.

How many people are there like Paris Hilton, Britney Spears, or Howard Hughes who ended up in misery trying to fill their Well Within with the contentment of wealth and recognition?

How many celebrities are there like Tiger Woods, Michael Jackson, or Marilyn Monroe who, as far as the rest of the world was concerned, *had it all*. All the money, all the fame, all the attributes to give them contentment. Still, the Well was empty. More and more conquests sadly failed to fill the contentment needs of the Well Within.

Please listen to me; this is the big answer:

THERE IS ONLY ONE WAY FOR YOU TO FILL THE WELL WITHIN.

God created you with an empty Well Within for the express purpose of filling it with Himself.

True contentment and joy come only when you fill your wonderful Well Within with the love of God.

Not wealth.

Not lust.

Not drugs and alcohol.

Not stuff.

Only God's love, invited by you into your Well Within, will give you what you have always been looking for. That's when you'll find yourself overflowing with contentment and joy.

That's when you can thankfully say, "I have arrived."

I'd like to illustrate this point with a sad but true story that has a happy ending.

THE RISE AND FALL OF STRAW

Darryl Strawberry was paid millions of dollars to do what he loved to do most—to play baseball; he had all the "stuff" anyone could ever want: houses, cars, and fame; legions of adorning fans; and ladies who fell all over him.

Yet, within his six-foot-six frame Darryl had a deep Well Within starving for contentment. In the recesses of his mind he was still a frightened little boy in Crenshaw, California, awaiting his father's punishment.

"You're no good, boy, you'll never amount to nothin'," repeated his drunken father, raising the strap to inflict another stinging welt on Darryl's back.

More painful than the beatings were the hurtful words that were indelibly pounded into his mind. He was worthless—there was no reason to believe otherwise, and that fostered a self-loathing that would spread like metastasizing cancer for years to come.

Few would argue that Darryl Strawberry was one of the greatest baseball players ever born. He rose to great heights; an eight-time All-Star player with four World Series rings. Yet his life story, told magnificently in the book *Straw*, is one of the saddest you've ever read.

He uses a metaphor to describe it.

"Picture a man falling down a long, long flight of steps. Bang. Crash. He falls and falls, head over heels. Sometimes he throws out his hands, grabs the railing, slows his fall for an instant. But, momentum, gravity, and his own weight are against him. He keeps crashing down those steps, down and down and down. Until finally he lands at the very bottom. Cut, bruised, broken, his head swimming, he lies there flat on his back. It's only then that he can begin to rise up again. Get himself back on his feet. Stand there looking up that long, long flight of stairs and think, 'How did I survive that?' That was me,"[1] he says.

Could Darryl Strawberry possibly climb back up? Could he take the God-given gifts he was born with, and his mother's conviction that he had a greater purpose, and pull himself back up those stairs, to a life with meaning and joy?

Well, come along. And hang on for the ride.

Right from the beginning Darryl Strawberry knew he was special.

"I knew I had natural athletic talent from when I was maybe ten years old," he says. "I was good at every sport . . . while I was playing I could almost forget my anger and my troubles."[2]

While his father was a raging alcoholic who never offered fatherly support or guidance, his mother, Ruby, was a rock; she raised him along with his two brothers and two sisters. A remarkably pretty woman, she had a quiet yet strong spirit. Always telling Darryl to "get up and go. God is gonna get the good outta you."

But it was a little league coach, John Mosely, who became the first substitute father figure to inspire him.

"He pushed me, pulled me . . . made me believe in myself,"[3] remembers Darryl. "I made a little sign and stuck it on the door of the bedroom: I AM GOING TO THE MAJORS. My sisters thought I was crazy. My mom didn't pay it much mind. She just saw that I was happy playing ball. She supported me, but never pushed."[4]

When he was an eighteen-year-old high school senior, his baseball playing began to capture attention and *Sports Illustrated* called him a "black Ted Williams." They said, "He's lanky, he's long, he's smooth . . . just like Ted Williams."

The next decade and a half was an astonishing journey for Darryl; up those stairs and down, in a series of—BOOM—ups, and—SLAM—downs.

An early BOOM was when another coach told him, "You're the number one pick in the nation . . . drafted by the New York Mets!"[5]

Suddenly the New York media was clamoring to talk with him.

"All the attention just made me feel uncomfortable," he recalls, "I just wanted to play baseball . . . I was still so shy, so full of self-doubt and even self-hate. I may have been a big, tall strapping lad, but inside I was one scared little rabbit."[6]

Darryl's quest to find contentment to fill his Well Within led him to start filling it with all the wrong things, right from his first season with the Mets.

"I began to sow the wild oats of my own destruction. To put it bluntly, I took my first steps that year toward becoming an alcoholic and drug addict"[7]—SLAM.

Contrary to what we might think, the fame and adoration of being a big-league ballplayer had an opposite effect on Darryl.

"Once I was walking in New York City with my mom," he said. "We passed a homeless guy huddled on the sidewalk and I told my mom I envied him. 'Why on earth would you say that?' she asked. 'Because if I was like him, I wouldn't have to worry about everybody pulling at me . . . nobody would pay any attention to me at all.' That's how I felt. The notoriety is a pain. You can't go anywhere without people tugging at you."

Meanwhile his rocketing ascent as a Mets star was just beginning. Although the team had a dismal season in '83, finishing twenty-two games out, "I'd done well personally," he says.[8] BOOM.

Women were at his beck and call, and one in particular, Lisa, became his girlfriend. He said he loved her. Yet, like so many of his teammates, he conveniently rationalized that cheating was okay. And as loving as their relationship may have been at times, it grew more and more acrimonious.

"My stormy relationship with Lisa did not help my performance on the field, either,"[9] he admits.

SLAM, he slipped into a slump.

"You're no good, boy, you'll never amount to nothin'." His father's echoing words seemed to be validated by the fans and the sports writers.

"With everyone telling me that I was letting the team down, my feelings got intensely hurt. Midway through the season I was dragging myself reluctantly to the park. I didn't feel like taking the abuse again. I had already learned that drinking was one way to cope with my problems. I just hadn't learned that it was one terrible way to do it."[10]

He became frustrated with the media. They'd built him up since he was in high school, "the black Ted Williams, the next Willie Mays, the new Reggie Jackson," yet never allowed him to have a slump. "Just playing very well was never enough for them. I was supposed to amaze and stupefy every time I went to the plate."

At the time he couldn't understand why he was treated so differently. Only much later did he comprehend that he had a certain "X factor," and his love-hate relationship with the fans and the press actually sold tickets.

"I'd step up to the plate and the entire stadium, tens of thousands of people, were rooted to their seats. Nobody moved . . . nobody got up and headed for the bathroom when Straw was on deck. They might be chanting 'Dar-ryl, Dar-ryl,' Dar-ryl' . . . or they might be screaming 'you stink' . . . but they did not move . . . no one wanted to miss whether I struck out or put the ball in orbit. Whatever it was, they wanted to be there to see it."

It was a Mets batting coach who counseled him not to let the media or the fans get inside his head.

Eventually he built himself a mental armor. He began manipulating the crowd.

"When I went into a slump . . . my attitude was, 'Oh, you're gonna boo me? Okay, I'm gonna hit two home runs today.' I'd go up to bat—they're booing me—pow. Hit my first one off the scoreboard. The place erupts. Next time I go up to bat they're like statues. You could hear a kernel of popcorn drop. I slam another out over the left field wall. The joint goes nuts. Thirty thousand fans fly up like they're all in ejector seats. The roar is deafening."[11]

With a sense of satisfaction, he reflects, "If you let them inside your head you're done. You have to learn how to turn it back on them." Then he quietly adds, "From growing up under my father, I had lots of practice ignoring abuse."[12]

When Lisa told him she was pregnant, he wrestled with what to do. His brain told him that he should marry the girl, for he certainly didn't want to become the kind of father his own father had been to him. But his heart was sending another message.

"On the day of the wedding I felt like a man on his way to the electric chair," he recalls. He drove around and around with his friend not knowing what to do.[13]

"You gotta go through with it," said his friend. "The invitations have been sent out. Everyone's at the church waiting for you."

How many of us can identify with Darryl's conflict? We want to do the right thing but know it's the wrong thing? How many bad choices have we made hearing ourselves or others tell us it's the "right thing" to do?

Darryl showed up an hour late. And married the mother of his child.

That year Darryl Strawberry played a key role on the team that climbed from the bottom to become known as "The Amazing Mets." BOOM. In 1986, they were the winningest team in baseball. And they did it in the most boisterous manner.

"We played to dominate, crush, conquer and humiliate every other team in baseball. We won 108 games. No team would beat that record until the 1998 Yankees—and I would be on that team, too. We finished the season leading the East by an awesome 21 games. We were the cockiest and most obnoxious, too."[14]

Postgame partying kicked up a notch. "We were bad enough before, but '86 was the season our lifestyle . . . including my consumption of speed . . . got way out of hand,"[15] he admits.

Darryl's normal demeanor was quiet and polite. He was Dr. Jekyll. But that all changed when he got a few beers in him. "I got nasty and obnoxious, and my Mr. Hyde popped out. All my anger, my frustrations with my personal life and marriage, my constant feelings of self-doubt, all the stuff I thought I was drinking to repress, it would just come out."

His on-field performance was soaring. But—SLAM—his off-field life was crashing.

"I was playing the best ball of my career. But my personal life was a shambles. I was depressed, lonely and frustrated at home and brought the baggage with me to the park."[16]

That was evidenced in his deteriorating relationship with Lisa.

"'Who were you talking to?' I hollered.

"Lisa's defense was offense. 'Stop shouting! You're drunk.'"

"I raised my hand and smacked her across the face. Hard. I broke her nose with the heel of my hand."

As bad as that day turned out, another was worse. The day that Lisa read in the paper that a woman had filed a paternity suit against her husband.

"Pretty soon we were screaming at the top of our lungs," says Darryl. "Something exploded in me. My rage at her, and at myself, my shame, my frustration, all of it boiling . . . I swung my fist and punched her in the head.

"She grabbed some kind of metal rod . . . a fireplace poker and was swinging at me. I ran to a closet where I kept a .25 pistol. As Lisa charged me, swinging that rod, I turned, raised my arm and pointed that pistol right at the bridge of her nose. She froze.

"Her mother chose that moment to emerge from her room. Her hands flew to her mouth. She ran out of the room and called 911."[17]

Minutes later police officers were pounding on the door. Darryl was taken away in handcuffs and had his first arrest, for possession of an unlicensed handgun.

Things had come full circle with his father. "Now I was the big, violent, raging drunk who'd threatened his wife with a gun."[18]

Once again Darryl was that guy whom he'd imagined falling and falling down a long flight of stairs, more and more out of control. Crash. Bang. SLAM.

Only through the clarity of hindsight can he now see that he was operating in two different worlds that were never going to be compatible. "Baseball isn't life. It's a game. There are clear rules and regulations. The paths and lines are all straight and well-marked. Life isn't like that at all. Life is chaos and confusion. It's much harder to figure out."[19]

Only now can he see the toxic outcome of trying to fill the Well Within with fame, money, lust, and substances.

"I see these young celebrities today, a Britney Spears or a Lindsay Lohan . . . and my heart goes out to them," he reflects.[20] "The really sick thing is the way the media not only expects these young people to screw up and do something stupid or scandalous, they push them into it."[21] As for him, he still had had a long distance to fall down that long staircase in his metaphor, with a SLAM downward for every BOOM upward.

The Mets grew impatient with his off-field antics and gave him a take-it-or-leave-it offer. Because his on-field performances were still those of a champion, the Dodgers were willing to pick him up, never fully knowing the depth of turmoil below the surface.

"All I can tell you is that I was in great pain, and the drinking and drugs brought me some temporary relief. But, I'll say it again: all the fame, all the success, all the money in the world don't add up to a thing if you're hurting in your soul. It does no good to have millions of people and all that press telling you who you are, when you haven't figured that out yet for yourself. At the height of my career, I just signed a huge contract with the Dodgers, more than $20 million over five years, but who am I as a person? I didn't know."[22]

·   ·   ·

Are you understanding the point of this story? That we are born with a craving for contentment. No matter how old and how successful we are, there is still a little infant somewhere inside us who wants to be picked up and cradled by a loving parent. For a boy, there's a particular desire to seek the contentment that comes from approbation by a loving father. When we are deprived of that, we seek other ways to fill our Well Within with contentment.

Darryl's brother Michael seemed to have plenty of contentment. Everyone could see the difference between the two of them. Michael had joy. He wasn't rich and famous, he was a cop, but he was truly happy. That's because Michael had stepped out of the shadows of his life, and into the light. He'd gotten right with God.

"Michael had been saved," says Darryl. "He'd say to me, 'Man you got to get your life together.'"

He also remembers thinking, "I could use some happiness. Not the fake happiness that comes from drinking, or drugs, or fame or sex. True happiness in my soul, the happiness that comes from being at peace with yourself."[23]

That's when he finally went along with his brother's urgings and attended a church service with an old-time preacher, Morris Cerullo.

"When Morris Cerullo spoke it felt like he was speaking directly to me. 'You're searching,' he said. 'God has called you here for a reason. You're here for a purpose.'"[24] That struck a chord with Darryl because it was similar to what his mom had always told him: "You got a call on your life."

Darryl surprised himself by standing up and joining a long line of people going up to Morris Cerullo. It was a transformational moment.

"He looks into my eyes . . . but he isn't speaking to me. He's speaking to an evil spirit inside me. 'Oh no, demon, you gotta come out of here,'" he remembers the pastor passionately saying. "He laid his hands on me. Bam! The power of God hit me like a lightning bolt, and I fell right down on the floor.

"Maybe you've seen evangelists on TV lay their hands on people, and you think, 'It's fake. Those people are acting. They've been coached.' Well, all I can tell you is that nobody coached me, and I wasn't faking a thing. What I felt was absolutely real, a physical force, and it truly knocked me to the floor. The best way I can describe the feeling is that it was like a roaring river pouring though me. Even after I stood back up I could feel it flowing through me."[25]

That was another—BOOM—another upbeat moment in his life, but it didn't change things the way we might expect.

"Accepting God into your life—feeling that power rush through you—isn't the end. Your life doesn't suddenly become all peace and quiet. All hell broke out in my life from that point on," he says, warning of the spiritual warfare that often unfolds.

His next career pothole was injury and being placed on the disabled list for several weeks.

"Here I was struggling to get it right . . . and I hurt myself a month into the season. When doubts started creeping into my mind . . . I just thought, 'What's the point? Maybe I need to go back to my old ways.' And I did. That's what substance abusers do. Any justification to keep using."[26]

"God came calling. But I pretended I wasn't home. I hid," he says.

Darryl managed to come back after the All-Star break and—BOOM—started playing again. He slammed twenty-eight homers and knocked in ninety-nine RBIs. "If I hadn't injured myself, it might have been my best season ever."

Off the field, though, the madness continued: "I was a full-blown alcoholic and using crack. It was ugly."

By 1994 Lisa had divorced him, and his new girlfriend was pregnant. True to form, they fought. In one of their biggest fights ever, he hit her. "My pregnant girlfriend. The woman I loved. I was under arrest again."

Before long, another SLAM, the IRS investigated him for tax fraud.

Dodgers manager Tommy Lasorda blasted Darryl in the media as the Dodgers dropped him.

SLAM, again.

Still, Darryl's talents were so extraordinary that teams seemed to believe that the risk was worth it. The Giants were next to take it. But they hedged their bet by making a deal to hire Darryl's brother Michael as well. It made a lot of sense.

"Officially he was a batting practice pitcher," says Darryl, "but his real job was to keep an eye on me. He had to quit his LAPD job . . . but he was excited about it . . . back to his first love, baseball, after a decade on the police force." He adds, "I loved having Mike with me. We did everything together. We slept in adjacent rooms. We prayed together. We talked a lot."

Things were looking rosy. BOOM.

Then, that August, SLAM, the Major League Baseball players went on strike and Darryl was idle again.

But another SLAM hit him harder. His fifty-five-year-old mother was diagnosed with breast cancer. "She was our rock. It was Mom who always said, 'You will come out of this on the other end.'"

Next, he decided to go ahead and plead guilty on those tax charges. SLAM. He was fined $350,000, and sentenced to six months probation and home confinement.

A while later a routine drug test showed cocaine in his urine. SLAM. The commissioner of baseball suspended him for sixty days.

As far as the Giants were concerned, that was it. They fired him. SLAM.

You're no good, boy, you'll never amount to nothin'. His father's words seem truer and truer.

"With everything going on, I slipped back into drinking and drugging," says Darryl.

It makes you wonder how many BOOMS and SLAMS, ups and downs, a person can take in life. Yet, for all the times that Darryl Strawberry gave up on himself in his quest to fill the Well Within—in a desperate search for contentment—God never gave up on him. Never once. He was always right there, with an outstretched hand, offering to pull him back up as he tumbled and tumbled down those stairs. And, just as He does in each of our lives, God Divinely Aligned people and events in Darryl's life at just the right time.

He "just happened" to meet a new agent, a hardworking fellow named Bill Goodstein, who was able to get to the Yankees' famous owner George Steinbrenner, convincing him to give Darryl yet another chance. BOOM.

"George picked me up when everyone else in the world was saying, 'No no no, he's too much trouble, he's through.' George didn't care what anyone said. He thought I deserved a chance to bounce back."

Darryl was determined, this time, to make it work. "There was always a champion inside me ready to rise to the challenge if only I would let him. So, once again, I cleaned up my act,"[27] he says.

He was keeping it together, but in his words, "the cracks were still there. I had just taped over them. And the next shocks were still to come."

His wonderful new agent, Bill Goodstein, who he was beginning to think was an angel, died of a heart attack. At fifty-six.

SLAM, SLAM.

Within days his mom died.

"I yelled at God . . . then, I crawled into bed and didn't get up for a couple of weeks."[28]

In a short time he had lost the man who he believed could rescue his career, and his mom, the one person he could always turn to for unconditional love. And then, says Darryl, "Just to make sure my will was at my lowest . . . the Yankees decided not to bring me back in '96. I was crushed."

SLAM again.

Losing a friend or a job is one thing, but as I said earlier, losing a parent is something none of us is ever prepared to experience. Until they are gone we don't begin to understand the depth of the foundation that they have created for us. Nor do we fully appreciate the power of the words they did, or didn't, say. We usually remain in a state of bewilderment and uncertainty for weeks, never quite comprehending that the person who once lifted us up, hugged us, and provided our Well Within with temporary contentment can never do it again.

Darryl was mired in mourning for days and days until, somewhere down deep, the memory of his mother's voice finally got him up. "She told me before her passing that God was going to get out of me what he had called me to do. I could hear her saying, 'Get up and go. You can run, you can hide, but he's gonna get it out of you.'"[29]

As Darryl pulled himself from his bed and began moving in a positive direction, God provided another Divine Alignment. Just the right person entered his path.

Bill Goodstein's son-in-law, Eric Grossman, stepped in and picked up the reins. He convinced Darryl to play for the St. Paul Saints, a team consisting of players who'd fallen out of the system and wanted to revive their careers. The idea was downright offensive, at first. *Darryl Strawberry? A champion? Playing ball with has-beens?* But, once he accepted the truth, he went to St. Paul and played well. So well that one day a call came in: "The Yankees want you back."

BOOM.

But stand by. It's time for another SLAM.

The doctor told him, "You have a tumor in your colon the size of a walnut. It's inflamed . . . blocking your colon, which is why you've been in such pain. And, it may be malignant. Cancer."[30]

For a man whose life had been a cascading series of ups and downs—BOOMS and SLAMS—Darryl's resolve, once again, cracked. After four years of sobriety, he reached for a drink.

"As every alcoholic knows, you can't have just one. It's no twelve-step cliché. That first drink throws open all the alcoholic switches in your body and your brain, and instantly you're drinking again like you never missed a day."[31]

Yet, believe it or not, people stood by him.

"George Steinbrenner stuck by me, when everybody in the country was howling at him to fire me."[32]

George didn't really have to. Because it was the commissioner of baseball's suspension of Darryl for 120 days, after his trial for possession of cocaine resulted in a plea of no contest, that finally ended his career in baseball, once and for all.

SLAM, and more SLAMS.

The cancer was confirmed. And it was spreading.

Darryl Strawberry was still falling and falling down those metaphoric stairs.

Surgery removed the cancer, but when he broke his probation, he was sentenced to eighteen months in prison.

"I sat in the cell that night and thought about how I'd come to this place in my life. Darryl Strawberry, eight-time All-Star, four World Series rings, sitting in a jail cell, headed to a Florida state prison."[33]

Yet, in retrospect, he looks upon that experience philosophically.

"I believe God protected me from myself . . . I was sick and crazy out of my mind, doing all kinds of crazy things, so there was no way to protect myself. So . . . God says, 'Well, I'll lock him up in prison and protect him from himself. Maybe that'll be the starting point to his getting his life together.' And, it worked."[34]

Then, after prison—BOOM—perhaps the most important

Divine Alignment in Darryl's life: he went to a Narcotics Anonymous recovery convention where he met Tracy Boulware.

He was captivated by her right away, her beauty inside as well as outside, and was drawn to her confident demeanor. And she wasn't doing flip-flops over his fame.

Early in their conversation he was candid about his faith. "What do you think about Jesus? Because I love Him. Would that be a problem for you?"

She laughed. "Me, too."[35]

Having gotten herself straight a year earlier, Tracy was further along her journey than Darryl. She was involved in her church and into the power of the Word.

Soon they were seeing each other regularly, and Tracy was establishing boundaries.

"I don't care how many home runs you've hit. That's not going to do anything for us living happily ever after. Forget the old Darryl. You have to find out who you are now," she said.

"Little by little, step by step, she dragged me down the path to getting right. It was a huge ordeal for both of us. I was really trying. My wild and stupid behavior was finally sputtering out," says Darryl. She told him, "If I can get clean, you can," adding, "Let's find a simple life for us."

Darryl committed himself to that objective. He flew back to California and spent six months in a spare bedroom at his sister Regina's home. He says he felt like a "monk in a cave."

"Regina and the kids were practically the only people I saw. I barely left my room, except to go to church. I read and studied the Bible with the same intense focus I used to devote to playing ball. I read until late at night, with the Bible on my chest as I went to sleep."

He taught himself to pray. Really pray. Not just dispassionately saying some words, but truly humbling himself before God, in complete surrender, asking for God's help.

"Surrender means doing a lot of things you don't want to, and not doing a lot of things your desires tell you to," says Darryl. "I swore off all liquor, drugs and all sex. I had gotten used to thinking I needed all those things—needed them to fill the empty places inside me. We think we need all these things around us to make us happy. When you strip it all away you never miss it. There was no joy in it. God had to take it all away for me to realize that.

"I had raged through my life like a hurricane," he concludes. "And now, by sitting quietly studying, praying and purifying myself, I let the hurricane blow itself out."[36]

As he sat alone in that bedroom at his sister's house, Darryl unshackled himself from every excuse. "My father is no excuse. My childhood is no excuse. My self-loathing is no excuse," he confessed.

Finally, he was that man who had fallen all the way down those stairs. He was flat on his back. The only place to look was up.

"This time when God called, I didn't run away. I answered," he says.

At last his father's forecast was going to be proven false. *You're no good, boy, you'll never amount to nothin'.*

At last his mother's wishes were about to be realized. *Get up and go. God is gonna get the good outta you.*

At last, Darryl's Well Within began to fill to the top with contentment. He felt an overwhelming joy. He finally understood that the wonderful Well Within is intended to be filled with one thing, and one thing only. The love of God.

DARRYL AND TRACY'S POSTSCRIPT

Darryl and Tracy started that new simple life.

"A team of equal partners . . . committed to our relationship and to our faith," says Darryl.

They are dedicated to their various ministries, including work with autistic children. And Darryl particularly loves speaking to young people, hoping to help them avoid the whirlpool of destruction that he was sucked into.

"You don't have to hit rock bottom . . . like I did . . . before you can deal with your problems," he tells them, promising, "God has a role for each of you."[37]

We can learn from Darryl's experience, grateful that he did all the heavy lifting. But, just to drill home the point of his message, let's see it from a slightly different perspective . . . not the poor kid who grew up in Crenshaw, but the rich kid who grew up in Connecticut. Eric.

ERIC'S SEASON OF DISCONTENT

According to the old adage, Eric Gorman was born "with a silver spoon in his mouth." His dad was a well-to-do doctor and entrepreneur. He was wanting for nothing material. And if there was something he did want, he was provided the impetus to get it.

"If you can conceive it, you can achieve it; that's what my dad taught me," says Eric.

When he went off to college, Eric was guided by what he calls the three Gs: "Gold, Glory, and Girls." He seemingly was well positioned to obtain all three. He was tall, handsome, and gifted on the tennis court. And he drove a snappy BMW his family gave him for graduation.

Eric was highly motivated and committed. But he was different from his pal Luke. During high school, both had quests to do well at tennis, both hired private tennis coaches, and both worked hard. But Luke was a believer in someone up there bigger than himself, someone who served as his personal guidance system. Eric had none of that. He was going to become a tennis star on his own, and he was ready to walk, climb, or run over anyone who got in his way.

"We both played tennis at the same university," says Eric, "but I didn't realize that Luke had been counseled to keep his distance from me when we were in high school. His coach thought I'd be a bad influence on him."

But when Eric's life began to fall apart in college, it was Luke who stepped up to give him support.

"I had alienated everyone on the tennis team," he says. "Then things began to spiral downward; I sprained my ankle and realized I was no longer of value to my college tennis coach. Within a few weeks, my girlfriend dumped me and I wrecked my BMW—I was a picture of discontent."

He remembered that famous line from Jack Nicholson: "What if this is as good as it gets?"

It started adding up for him that no matter how much he had, he was discontented.

Looking thoughtful, Eric recalls his discovery: "Luke was the only one on my team who befriended me."

Eric began to follow Luke from darkness into the light, seeing a different way to approach life. He began to see a pathway to contentment that comes from experiencing God's love, joy, and peace; he attended Bible study.

Then, through words written by another Luke, centuries earlier, Eric found what he was looking for: contentment.

All he had to do was "Love the Lord your God with all your heart and with all your soul and with all your strength and with all your mind" (Luke 10:27) (NIV).

Today, tennis is still an important part of Eric Gorman's life.

"Tennis allows me to connect relationally with kids and adults and it opens doors for me to share my story of finding contentment in Jesus Christ.

"I'm married to an amazing lady, and every day I feel the joy of doing whatever God wants me to do. That's contentment!" he says.

ARRIVE!

You have a choice, of course. You can go right on trying to fill the Well Within with all kinds of things that provide you with fleeting contentment. Things that remind you of the contentment you felt from your mother's hug, or the acclaim you enjoyed for a childhood accomplishment. You may seek continued contentment by stuffing the Well Within with food, drugs, or alcohol. Perhaps lustful quests. You may acquire a bigger house and fill it with lots of stuff, with the flashiest car outside. But, as Darryl Strawberry and Eric Gorman attest, your Well Within was made to be filled by the Maker Himself. Until you do that, you'll never arrive at that place of peace and joy that you seek.

GPS STEP 7

GRATEFULLY ARRIVE WITH
A FULL WELL WITHIN

Once you fill the wonderful Well Within with God's Love, you'll reach destinations in accord with God's purpose for you. Express gratitude for your arrival, and ask your GPS Navigator what He wants you to do next.

WHAT'S NEXT?
THE ULTIMATE ARRIVAL

Once you've traveled the varied pathways of your life to arrive at a peaceful time and place where you get up every morning feeling great because your joyful relationship with God led you to contentment and happiness, you may ask, "What's next?"

Stories I've shared with you in this book have suggested that this is not the end at all, but only the beginning, that the "end of life" here on earth is merely the starting point for Your Ultimate Arrival.

Heaven or hell.

The map of your life, as seen from above, may look like a long, long railroad track across the horizon of time; there are lots of twists and turns, ups and downs, mountains and valleys, and like any map there are thousands of little sidetracks running off it. Upon a closer look you see that one rail travels in the darkness, the other in the light, and all along you've been able to choose which one you would travel by—darkness or light. Finally, the long railroad track culminates at a distinct junction. There's a signpost. One sign points to *HEAVEN*. The other to *HELL*.

Many people think that when you arrive at that junction, the decision about which path you'll be taking will not belong to you at all, but that God will be choosing which path you take. Not entirely so, according to my valued spiritual guide and friend Jeff Winter. He counsels, "God doesn't *send* anyone to Hell . . . We send ourselves by rejecting God's indescribable love and forgiveness for all our foul-ups and transgressions."

"God doesn't send anyone to Hell . . . We send ourselves."

In other words, you need to get your ticket to heaven through a decision you make prior to and/or at that final junction. I'll elaborate on this later.

For the moment let's just assume you're leaning back in your seat thinking, *Well, it appears that there's a fifty-fifty chance that what is being said here is right.* So, hedging your bet, you make the appropriate decision, get your ticket, and you place yourself on the pathway toward heaven.

That being the case, you start to wonder what you might expect to find. Let's take a look.

WHAT IS HEAVEN LIKE?

Heaven remains a distant concept.

People say it exists; you have no reason to doubt them—other than your own modest intellect, which sometimes gets in God's way—but bottom line, you really wish there was something more concrete—real evidence to *convince* you that heaven is *really* there. Am I right?

The Bible doesn't talk extensively about heaven. We are told of an indescribable place of peace: "Eye hath not seen, nor ear heard . . . the things which God hath prepared for them that love him."[1] And that those of us who have committed ourselves to Him can "rejoice, because your names are written in heaven."[2]

We are given comfort, that "there shall be no more death . . . sorrow, nor crying, neither shall there be any more pain."[3]

Jeff Winter says, "We always think of heaven as *up,* but that doesn't mean heaven is out there in space somewhere. *Up* means *higher* than anything you'll experience on earth; *beyond* anything you can imagine; or *above* any pain or temptation confronting you in this life.

"What kind of place is heaven?" asks Jeff rhetorically. "It's a place where we will have a new body." He pauses a beat, relishing his next statement: "There are no health clubs in heaven, because our bodies will be perfect."

For confirmation he quotes Paul: "We will be changed . . . in a flash, in a twinkling of an eye . . . the dead will be raised imperishable and we will be changed."[4]

"I believe we'll recognize each other," continues Jeff. "We'll just look the best we've ever looked. Flawless. The blind will see and the crippled will walk."

Does that mean there's no suffering in heaven? Well, according to Paul, who, in the Bible, was beaten, stoned, whipped, imprisoned, shipwrecked, and left for dead, "the sufferings of this present time are not worthy to be compared to the glory that shall be revealed in us."

Jeff interprets that this way: "God will make whole every aching heart, He'll heal every emotional wound, and He'll remove every tear duct because you won't need them anymore; sadness will be gone—you'll be joyful for all eternity."

The Bible provides this description of heaven: "There is a great city with . . . light like unto a stone most precious . . . clear as crystal . . . with no need of the sun, neither of the moon, to shine in it: for the glory of God did lighten it . . . there shall be no night there."[5]

Jeff expands on this passage: "There will be no darkness in heaven because we won't need to hide in the darkness."

Having digested these thoughts, I began to wonder how the Bible's promises about heaven might compare with the experiences of people who say they have *already visited* heaven—people who have had a "near death experience"—who technically die—then come back to life on earth.

LIFE AFTER LIFE: A STUDY

A quarter of a century ago there was a medical doctor, Raymond Moody, who became fascinated with the similar accounts of people he met who had been pronounced clinically dead. Dr. Moody set out to research the matter, and over several years he identified 150 cases of people who had what he labeled "near-death experiences." That was the first time the term was used. Today, references to "NDEs" are common in the language of those who study this field.

"What has amazed me since the beginning of my interest," wrote Dr. Moody, "are the great similarities in the reports, despite the fact that they come from people of highly varied religious, social, and educational backgrounds."[6]

Dr. Moody found that there were about "fifteen separate elements which recur again and again."

I have integrated Dr. Moody's list of similarities with those that I have distilled from stories in this book, arriving at the following commonalities that can help you compare one story to another.

People who believe that they have witnessed heaven, even though they may or may not have been officially declared dead, often experience some or all of the following:

1. You are outside your physical body; perhaps in the same physical area; a spectator of yourself.
2. You enter darkness, feeling rapid movement through a tunnel, approaching a distant light.
3. You may notice you have a new body that is different from the one you remember, yet perfect; no pain or suffering.
4. A loving being of light greets you nonverbally; an absence of sorrow is replaced by love and joy.

5. It is never dark in heaven; brilliant lightness is believed to come from God.

6. You are greeted by friends and relatives who have been restored to look their best.

7. There are borders or a gate that is "pearly" with the look of "fish scales."

8. You hear intense, extraordinary music and/or singing—several compositions all at once.

9. There are bright, indescribable colors.

10. There are multiple angels with white wings.

11. You encounter God, whose face is not visible, and/or Jesus, with beautiful eyes.

12. You may be told to return, it's not your time, though you may prefer to stay because of the love and joy.

13. On earth you avoid telling others; it's hard to describe and you don't think they'll believe you. But you're no longer afraid to die.

14. You learn that prayers of friends and family on earth—sometimes many people—may determine whether you remain in heaven or return to earth.

15. You are no longer afraid to die.

NDE IN THIS BOOK

Against the backdrop of this list and Dr. Moody's research on near-death experiences, let's compare the similarities among stories I've told in this book; people who were clinically dead, nearly dead, or who experienced what they believed was a glimpse of heaven.

In Chapter 1 I shared the story of Don Piper, who was driving home from a conference when he came headlight to headlight with a massive eighteen-wheel truck that was in his lane, crushing his car, flattening the roof.

"The last thing I remember was driving onto the bridge and suddenly everything became dark.[7] Then I remember being at the gates of heaven, surrounded by people, and hearing music."

By all accounts, Don died instantly. He was declared dead by at least four eyewitnesses.

You'll recall that the incessant prayers of a passerby, Dick Onerecker, was a key factor in Don's revival after an hour and a half.

Yet, as he later wrote in an immensely bestselling book, *Ninety Minutes in Heaven*, he saw old friends and relatives with new bodies, looking the best they'd ever looked: namely, a grandmother who had lost her teeth on earth had a magnificent smile in heaven; his grandfather shook his hand with a hand that was no longer missing fingers; and men who had been bald had full heads of hair.

He saw huge pearly-looking gates, reflecting pulsating light, and no artificial light, for God illuminated everything.

He said, "The music was my most precious memory of heaven . . . thousands of songs at the same time. I could distinguish each one with my heavenly ear."

Visually it was "a buffet of sight, sound, and aroma."

He had a joyful sense of euphoria and didn't want to return.

Another story focused on the experience of sixteen-year-old Nathan Christensen, victim of a horrible auto accident, who was exposed to freezing temperatures for two or more hours and subsequently slipped into a coma for several days. He was given a 1 percent chance of survival but was never officially declared clinically dead. In the coma he described a "vision." He saw an unusually bright light and had the sense that God leaned down, placed His head on his shoulder, and hugged him. He came out of the coma shortly thereafter.

Let's compare the similarities of these experiences with what happened to a lady named Cynthia Farrington, on Martha's Vineyard.

CYNTHIA—IT'S NOT YOUR TIME!

"I stopped breathing—I went through darkness—then there was a bright light, getting brighter and brighter, and I felt, 'I have to go toward it!' Then I could see her, my mother, up ahead of me!"

Squeezing her eyes as she spoke, Cynthia Farrington, slim, attractive, auburn-haired, was retelling a life-changing event of thirty years before. It was just as real today.

On that snowy January evening in 1981, at six forty-five, she was in the front seat of the car, nestled between John, her future husband, and a friend named Steve. The backseat was filled by a 125-pound German shepherd dog named Leif.

Suddenly they were jerking and lunging—the car skidding on a patch of ice; it was turning, twisting—crashing into a tree in a cacophony of screeching, grinding metal.

Without seat belts, the three were thrust forward, their heads smashing into the dashboard, but Cynthia fared the worst: the full weight of the dog, Leif, from the backseat, piled onto the back of her neck and shoulders, propelling her with still more force.

Everything went dark.

Time stopped for Cynthia.

John dragged himself from behind the wheel and got out of the car. Dazed, he looked around, then back into the crushed vehicle. Steve was injured, but moving. It was the sight of Cynthia that alarmed him. She was slumped over, not breathing!

An ambulance rushed Cynthia three miles to Martha's Vineyard Hospital in Oak Bluffs, Massachusetts, where she was subsequently airlifted during the night to Falmouth Hospital. She was admitted to intensive care and remained there for the next ten days, in a coma.

The MVH ER report at 7:35 p.m. states: "25 year old female in a motor vehicle accident . . . unconscious since time of accident, unresponsive to stimuli, having Cheyne-Stokes respirations, extremely

cold to touch and abrasions below left knee. An IV was started, intu-
bated due to difficulty breathing and Foley CD inserted."

It felt cold. It was dark.

As Cynthia walked toward the light, the darkness fell away. It
became warmer as the brightness became brighter and brighter.

She became aware of people walking on either side with her—
they seemed to be dressed in white—white robes—and they were
saying things.

What are they saying?

She was wrapped in a cocoon of safeness and peace.

I hear talking. Are those prayers?

She advanced.

The other people alongside seemed to be smiling, excited, looking ahead to the light.

And then Cynthia saw her!

"Mama! Wait! Wait for me."

Her mother's red hair billowed lightly as she stopped and turned.

Cynthia ran to her mother. Hugged her. She hugged her tightly,
not wanting to let her go. A feeling of protection and love washed
over her.

"No. You need to go back now. It's not your time!" her mother
said kindly, wiping away Cynthia's tears. "You still have things to
do."

Cynthia had not seen her mother since colon cancer had claimed
her life seven years earlier at age fifty; she was left with a memory of
her mother's deteriorated body. But now . . . she was radiant! She
looked beautiful! Her hair redder, standing out from her gown of
white.

"Wait for me, Mama! Please take me with you."

"No . . . not your time," repeated her mother.

But I want to stay, thought Cynthia, not understanding why she
couldn't.

All of a sudden the light began to fade and she again fell into darkness.

Not much of anything else can be remembered—her focus had been so drawn to her mother.

Were colors brighter in that realm? Was there music? She can't recall.

Doctors at Falmouth Hospital diagnosed a left temporal lobe contusion, bilateral basal skull fracture and right hemiplegia, prompting them to transport Cynthia to Newton-Wellesley Hospital outside of Boston for more specialized care. There she remained in a coma for some time longer, according to medical reports, "fully unresponsive for one month, then gradually woke up very lethargic and aphasic."

Cynthia's next awareness was from *within* the coma.

Take me home! That's what she wanted to say. But her eyes wouldn't open. Her lips failed to move. And her body was lifeless. *Get me out of here!*

It is often said that people in a coma can hear conversations that people are having around them and that weeks or months later they can recall them word for word.

Cynthia was amused when she heard her boyfriend, John, arguing with another man—a guy she had dated. Hospital policy dictated that only one person could enter an intensive care unit at a time. The two were loudly debating which one had the right to go in. John was the one likely to win, as he did on that day.

Thank God I'm in a coma, thought Cynthia, smiling in her thoughts.

After a while Cynthia began to slowly awaken, lethargic at first. Her challenges were both physical and emotional, initiating another transfer, this time to New England Rehabilitation Hospital, where she participated in a vigorous daily schedule of physical, speech, and occupational therapies.

The near-death experience—NDE—and her experience of entering into another realm were life changing for Cynthia.

Her mother's death had motivated her to pursue a career in nursing, but now she was consumed with a desire to help others even more.

"That's my purpose," she says with finality.

As a reflection of her new compassion and commitment, she spent three weeks helping Hurricane Katrina victims, and she has a highly unique ability to comfort patients who are on the threshold of death. She senses a peace coming over them just before they die, and when they depart—no longer afraid to die herself—she says, "I even feel an excitement for them."

Personally Cynthia found that her near-death tragedy elevated the importance of family, friends, and her beliefs. Love and gratitude are now easier to express.

Cynthia has been hesitant to share her story. That's not unusual among those who have had NDEs. And in accord with the select few, she says, "There are no words in our earthly language to describe what I saw and felt. But . . . I *do* know there is life after death."

Yet, you still wonder—your mind tells you that there is no way that these folks could have gotten together and compared notes to come up with similar descriptions of "the other side"—but what if their common experiences were somehow subconsciously drawn from some common information, something they've all read at some time in their lives?

Perhaps.

But what if the descriptions of heaven came from someone who hadn't been on earth long enough to be exposed to such information? Someone . . . like a child four to six years old?

Each of the three stories that follow, those of Akiane and Colton at age four, and of Alex at age six, reinforces the similarities we have noticed in the near death experiences or visions of adults discussed earlier.

THE CHILD WHO SPEAKS TO GOD

"Today I met God," whispered the sweet, blond-haired four-year-old.

"What's God?" replied her mother, Foreli, instantly puzzled; she had been an atheist all her life. She and her husband never spoke about religion, never prayed or went to church. Her children were homeschooled and didn't watch television.[8] In fact, Akiane—pronounced ah-kee-ah-nah—had never been out of her sight.

"God is light . . . and talks with me."

"Tell me about your dream."

"It wasn't a dream; it was real."

"So who is your God?" Foreli was caught between amazement and alarm that somehow someone had pierced the security of her home, putting wild ideas into her child's mind.

"I cannot tell you."

"Me? You can tell your own mom."

"The light told me not to," answered the child, with firmness.

"Why did you think it was God?"

"Just like I know you are my mommy and you know that I am Akiane."

Running off to play, Akiane left Foreli to ruminate about this conversation. She played it back, again and again, continually asking, *How could a child who never played pretend or created imaginary friends come up with these notions?* In fact, her daughter had no interest in fairy tales or fantasies of any sort.

Foreli says it was another six weeks before her daughter again spoke about God. "The smallest details, the prophetic speech, and the sense that she spent more time away in the spiritual world than with our family were hard to ignore. Sometimes she sounded like an older woman—not because of her voice, but because of her total sincerity, her strangely compelling comments, and her broad vocabulary. It scared us and inspired us at the same time."

Simultaneously Akiane began showing an intense interest in drawing. It was as if the four-year-old needed a means more than words to express what she was seeing in her visions, in her conversations with God.

"Sometimes she scribbled and sketched with her eyes closed . . . hundreds of figures and portraits on whatever surfaces she found . . . walls, windows, furniture, books, even her own legs and arms. I would find our white walls smeared with charcoal from our fireplace," says Foreli.

Additionally the child's reaction to music was perplexing.[9]

"She would start to cry every time any kind of music was played . . . she would beg us to stop the music. No one had the slightest idea why," Foreli continues. "One evening, I simply couldn't understand her, and I broke down, sobbing."

"Mommy, please don't cry," said Akiane. "I'm sorry. The music I hear in heaven is better than here. This music hurts my ears, but music in heaven is gentle . . . it feels like love . . . smells like flowers . . . dances like butterflies. Music there is alive! You can even taste it!"

Like living in a real-life mystery tale, Foreli and her husband, Markus, tried to understand their daughter's faith. They began venturing to different churches. It was a challenging time in their lives. They were nearly broke, yet the new-found faith budding in their family drew them to God.[10]

"For the first time in our lives we were experiencing indescribable joy, harmony, and peace," says Foreli.

•   •   •

"When I was four I had many visions of meeting God," says Akiane. "When I started drawing, God gave me ideas that I didn't even know what the meaning was, like the Pyramids. When I got a little older, I started knowing this was God—totally God—helping me with my art. He takes care of me like a butterfly."[11]

One morning, when Akiane was eight, her mother found her up early, gazing through the window.

"What are you doing?" asked her mother gently.

"I was with God again. I was told to pray continually. He showed me where He lived, and it was so light. He was whiter than the whites of whites. I was climbing transparent stairs; underneath I saw gushing waterfalls. As I approached my Father what impressed me the most were His gigantic hands. They were full of maps and events."[12]

"Then He told me to memorize thousands and thousands of wisdom words on a scroll that didn't look like paper, but more like intense light. And, in a few seconds, I somehow got filled up."

The young girl looked into her mother's wondering eyes.

"He told me that from now on I needed to get up very early and get ready for my mission."

"What mission?" asked her mother.

"When that time comes, you will see," said Akiane, closing the conversation for the moment.

One wonders if the mission Akiane was referencing was the one that captured her focus a short while later, at age nine: to reproduce on canvas, the image in her mind—the face of Jesus.

For weeks Akiane went to places like malls, parks, and street corners where she could stand and look at thousands of faces passing by. She was searching for someone whose facial features came close to the image of Christ that she had met in her mind.

She became more and more frustrated. So one day she asked her family to pray with her throughout the day.

"God, I need you to send me the right model . . . maybe it's too much to ask, but could you send him right through our front door?" she tearfully beseeched."[13]

Who on earth could have predicted the Divine Alignment that unfolded the very next day? The doorbell rang. It was an acquaintance of the family, a lady who said she thought that Akiane might like the features of the man she brought with her. A handsome, tall man smiled warmly at the young girl, and outstretched a strong hand.

Akiane was stunned that God would answer her prayer so promptly! And—right through the front door!

"This is he." Akiane blushed.

He was dressed in jeans, a white T-shirt, and old sneakers.

"What do you do?" Foreli asked.

"I'm a carpenter."

After he left, Akiane stayed in her room for several hours, overwhelmed with God's gift—the godwink of the promptly answered prayer. From memory, she began to sketch possible angles for her portrait.

Then, disappointment.

The carpenter telephoned. He apologized for disappointing her—he was honored—but felt unworthy to represent the image of Jesus.

Akiane refused to give up. For the next few days she repeated the fervent prayers that had caused God to send the carpenter in the first place. The next week she was overjoyed. He called back and said, "God wants me to do it."

Soon he was posing for Akiane as she took multiple photographs and studied his face, preparing for her marathon effort to replicate on canvas the image of Jesus she'd come to know. Over the next several days she stood at her canvas, intently focused, for forty hours. And to underscore her youth and innocence, almost oddly, it was a period when three of her baby teeth fell out.

"The process of her painting was incomprehensible," said her mother later. "It was as though the Almighty power was vibrating through her every vein."[14]

The portrait resembled the model, but Akiane altered features to reproduce the image of Jesus in her mind.

When she completed the portrait, she began immediately to prepare for a second painting of Christ, a profile of him looking up to heaven, with a focus on his strong hands.

Struggling to represent the hands, Akiane determined she needed more red, but ran out of paint. Her mother volunteered to quickly go to the paint store. But when she returned, it was the wrong shade of red. It failed to match the specific red that Akiane saw in her mind. Pricking her finger to produce a droplet of blood, she wiped it onto her mother's hand.

"This is the exact color I need," she said.[15]

Akiane had become uniquely attuned to colors. But, unlike colors we see, she was reproducing colors from her vision of heaven.

"The colors are out of his world," she says. "Hundreds and millions of more colors that we don't know yet."[16]

At the age of eight she completed her two most important paintings—the images of Christ.

"Like a bold light, he's pure; he's really masculine, he's strong and big. And his eyes are just beautiful."[17]

At this writing, Akiane is sixteen and paints prolifically with an ability that has led some to call her a child prodigy. Her paintings have sold for more than ten thousand dollars.

Yet, like any of us, she encounters roadblocks.

"Sometimes I'm frustrated . . . so I just start talking to God and He calms me down right away," says Akiane, adding thoughtfully, "Other people can have that feeling too."[18]

How can others communicate with God?

"The most important thing . . . is faith. Without faith you cannot communicate with God."

• • •

There is the story of another four-year-old, Colton Burpo, who experienced similar wonders of heaven, but who, unlike Akiane, was close to dying—perhaps did die—yet was never technically declared dead. The book detailing his extraordinary story, *Heaven Is for Real*,[19] written by his father Todd Burpo, has become a national bestseller.

A CHILD'S VIEW OF HEAVEN

"Daaadddeeee! Don't let them take me."[20]

The startling, spine-tingling scream from his nearly four-year-old son, as nurses pushed the gurney toward the operating room, put Todd's stomach and heart into a vise grip. A part of him wanted to rush forward to cradle Colton from any further harm, while another wanted to pull down the shades of his mind and surrender, helplessly letting the doctors have their way while he himself crawled into a fetal position.

He looked at his wife, Sonja, her face drawn and tear-stained, wiping away a wisp of dark disheveled hair, wishing she could wipe away this nightmare. Her lips were pouty, holding back cries of anguish as she punched the telephone to *do* something—to dial up as many prayer chains as possible.

Neither Todd nor Sonja could ever have prepared themselves for the horrendous two weeks they were about to face, or for the words and stories that would emerge from the lips of their child, startling them and everyone who heard them—words and stories about visiting heaven.

To allow his own pent-up emotions to escape, Todd looked around for a place to be alone. He slipped into a vacant examining room adjacent to the waiting area where Sonja had taken a seat.

"I just broke down. I was mad at God. I was just frustrated, fed up. And I remember telling him, 'God, after all I've done for you, and now you're gonna take my kid? Is this how you treat your pastors?'"[21]

Yelling at God was no way to pray, but at the moment he felt like pointing fingers.

A quick mind shift suggested a different thought. Maybe it *wasn't* God's fault—maybe it was *his*. He'd *told* the doctors at their small community hospital about his and Sonja's history with childhood appendicitis, but when they evaluated the matter for five hours—*five hours!*—perhaps he should have taken matters into his own hands sooner. Would his son stand a better chance to live right now if he, Todd Burpo, had made a head-of-the-family decision earlier—instead of continuing to trust the doctors in Imperial, Nebraska—and decided to take the hour-and-a-half drive to the Great Plains Regional Medical Center in North Platte?

"God, please help us. Don't let our son die." Todd buried his face in his hands, his shoulders rising and falling with his sobs.

In near desperation, he mentally raced over the time line. Once the X-rays had shown those three dark masses in his son's tiny torso, shouldn't people have jumped into action?

His mind replayed the panic of the first moment he saw the onset of death in his child's face. As a pastor, he'd seen it dozens of times, at hospice centers: graying skin and darkening around the eyes.

He reran in his mind his conversation with doctors in Imperial. "Are you sure it's not appendicitis? We have a family history." And his discomfort with their subsequent bewilderment: "That's not what the blood tests show."

He and Sonja *wanted* to trust the doctors. For crying out loud, the couple had no medical training. He was a pastor. She was a teacher. But what if he had grabbed authority earlier? Decided sooner to bring his child to this better-equipped medical center in North Platte? Would his child have been better attended for a ruptured appendix, saving wasted hours of poison seeping into his insides?

But let's thank God for blessings, he thought. Now, at least, Colton was in the hands of a doctor he knew and trusted, Dr. Timothy O'Holleran.

For his dear wife, Sonja, it had been a several-year period of crisis-mode praying. Right from the time she realized she was losing their second child, about two months into the pregnancy—a miscarriage. The world may soon gloss over an unseen baby, but not a mother. A mother knows that a human life, a child growing inside her, is now gone, along with all her hopes and dreams for that baby. Now, Colton was a gift from God. He was her little pal. The towheaded, blond, blue-eyed fireball.[22]

Determining it was time to surrender his self-imposed incarceration, to rail at God, Todd pulled himself from a slumped position, in order to be where he ought to be . . . belatedly hugging and comforting his wife. For the next ninety minutes or so they prayed together.

"Mr. Burpo?" It was a nurse.

"Yes," Todd said, looking up.

"Your son is out of surgery in recovery. He's screaming for you."[23]

Todd and Sonja jumped up and followed the nurse. In moments they intercepted Colton's gurney in the hallway on the way to ICU and placed kisses on his cheeks while whispering consoling words.

"Hi, Mommy. Hi, Daddy."[24]

Thank You, God! thought Todd. Colton looked pale, but the hint of a smile provided a moment of hope.

In the hospital room, Colton looked miniature in an adult bed. He waited patiently for the nurse to finish fussing with the tubes and bed height. There was something he wanted to say.

"Dad? Do you know I almost died?"[25]

Where did he hear that? Did he overhear the nurses? thought Todd, not quite knowing how to respond. *He'd been under anesthesia. And He and Sonja certainly wouldn't suggest the danger of death to their not-quite-four-year-old.*

It was seven more days in the hospital, with doctors and nurses continuing to drain the poison that had seeped through Colton's body, before the Burpos were told they could go home. But as Todd and Sonja were pushing Colton's balloon-decorated wheelchair toward the exit, Dr. O'Holleran intercepted them, shouting out, "You can't go!"[26]

A last-minute blood test had revealed a dangerous elevation in Colton's white cell count, and a CT confirmed that more surgery was required to clean out additional pockets of poison in his tummy.

Colton cried. Todd and Sonja wilted, tearing up, and feeling pummeled.

Another four days of tension—including a period when the doctor's decision to airlift Colton to a children's hospital in Denver was derailed by a massive snowstorm; it was another four days of an extraordinary outpouring of pleas from the dedicated prayer warriors at Todd and Sonya's church, where scores of worried friends gathered to cry out to God to save little Colton.

Finally, after seventeen days of battling despair, Colton was sitting up in bed playing with action figures as a steady stream of nurses at North Platte Medical Center peeked in at the little boy who was now labeled "the miracle child."

It was now clear that all the medical professionals had considered Colton nearly DOA—dead on arrival.

Aside from a couple of puzzling comments, it wasn't until four months later that Colton began making eye-widening statements about what had happened to him during his time in the hospital.

During a car ride through North Platte, en route to a family gathering, Todd kiddingly asked his son if he'd like to stop by the hospital for a visit.

"No, Daddy," was his quick response from his car seat in the back, next to his sister, seven-year-old Cassie. Then, without a hint of realizing the significance of his words, he added, "That's where the angels sang to me,"[27] said Colton. "Jesus and some angels came and flew me up to heaven."[28]

Todd and Sonja glanced at each other, baffled.

"Where was Jesus?" ventured Todd.

"I was sitting in his lap."[29]

Taking a deep breath, Todd looked at his mystified wife and suggested they pulled into an upcoming Arby's restaurant.

Musing over their sandwiches, Todd probed further.

"Colton, where were you when you saw Jesus?"

"At the hospital . . . when Dr. O'Holleran was fixing me," the boy replied, nonchalantly. "You were in a little room by yourself, praying, and Mommy was in a different room . . . praying and talking on the phone."[30]

"I hadn't told my wife about that prayer," said Todd. "I was upset; I was mad, embarrassed about it. And when my son could tell me where I was, and what I was doing while he was in surgery, I was caught completely off guard."[31]

Todd and Sonja were dumbfounded. Chewing their sandwiches became an activity to disguise astonishment.

"But you were in the operating room, how could you know what we were doing?" ventured Todd.

"I was looking down.[32] I could see doctors all around me. And you and Mommy in other rooms."

Sonja blinked rapidly.

Todd thought perhaps that was enough probing for one day. Better still, perhaps he and Sonja needed some time to process this and talk about it later.

When they were alone, Todd and Sonja traded looks of bewilderment.

"Do you really think he saw angels?"

"And Jesus?"

"I don't know."

"Was it a dream?"

"I don't know . . . he seems so sure."[33]

The question was, "How could a child—just turning four years old—make this up?"

Colton's revelations about his supposed visit to heaven began to emerge randomly and matter-of-factly. Sitting on the floor one day playing with toys, he pulled a plastic horse from a pile, held it up, and announced:

"Hey, Dad, did you know Jesus has a horse?"

"A horse?"

"Yeah, a rainbow horse. I got to pet him. There's lots of colors."

"Where are there a lot of colors, Colton?"[34]

"In Heaven, there's a lot of colors, a lot of people and animals."[35]

For the first time Todd comprehended that Colton was talking about not just having left his *body* at the hospital—he was talking about having left the *hospital itself*!

"You were in heaven?" Todd uttered, trying to remain composed.

"Well, yeah, Dad."

Todd processed the hair-raising things his boy had just told him. *Did our son die and come back? The medical staff never gave any indication of that happening.*[36]

He resolved to explore further, careful not to lead Colton in any way.

"What did Jesus look like?"

The little boy put down his toys and looked at his father earnestly. "He was wearing white robes with a purple stripe[37] and He has markers."

"Markers?" asked Todd, immediately thinking of crayons or Sharpies. "Like you color with?"

"Markers," Colton said emphatically, standing up, pointing at one palm, then the other. Then bending, pointing at his feet.[38] 'That's where Jesus's markers were Dad.'"[39]

"What color are they?"

"Red."

Todd, a pastor, knew, as every Christian knows, that Jesus was nailed to the cross, through the palms of his hands and through his feet, just where Colton was pointing.

He knew his four-year-old had never heard what he was describing, nor read about it in the Bible.

Later, when Todd was with Sonja, both parents were positive that neither had ever spoken to Colton about these kinds of things. *How could my little boy know this stuff?*[40] was the reoccurring thought crossing both of their minds.

For several weeks Todd and Sonja sifted through the tidbits of information coming from their boy's experience. They reexamined the medical records at North Platte Medical Center. There had been no official report that their son had been clinically dead during surgery. Todd had thought about how he was going to open up a dialogue with Colton on this matter.

"People have to die to go to heaven," he stated one day.

"I must have died, then," replied Colton calmly, "because I was there."[41]

As an afterthought, he continued: "Daddy, do you remember when I yelled for you at the hospital when I waked up?"[42]

How could Todd ever forget that nurse coming to him, saying his son was screaming for him. A confirmation that his little boy was still alive!

"I knew I was leaving Heaven because Jesus came to me and said, 'Colton, you have to go back.' Even though I didn't want to go back, he said he was answering my dad's prayer."[43]

It suddenly struck Todd, with shame, that his "prayer" included those angry moments alone in that examining room when he desperately railed at God as he worried, having seen the onset of death appearing on his little boy's face, if he would ever see his precious child alive again.

I remember that disrespectful, screaming prayer, he thought. And, *He's answering that prayer?*[44]

If he'd ever questioned it for a second, this was proof for him: God, the Navigator, answers prayers!

Riding in the car one day through Nebraska farmland, Colton made another surprising disclosure: "Dad, you used to have a grandpa named Pop, didn't you?"[45]

"Yep, sure did,"[46] said Todd, quickly assessing if he'd ever talked with Colton about his favorite grandfather who was killed in a car wreck before Todd himself turned seven.[47]

"'He's really nice," observed Colton, once again causing Todd's eyes to widen.

"'Really?"

"Yeah, you used to play with him as a kid."

"He had a dog," replied Todd, nodding, "we'd take him out and hunt rabbits."

"I know. Pop told me."[48]

Todd glanced at Colton in bewilderment as his son continued: "This guy comes up to me and says, 'Are you Todd's son?' I say 'yes,' he says, 'well, I'm his grandfather.'"[49]

"What did you and Pop do when it got dark?" asked Todd, not too coyly trying to get additional information.

"It never gets dark in heaven, Dad. It's always bright. God and Jesus light up heaven."[50]

That was enough for Todd to absorb for one day. But later on, sitting at the old desk that had once been Pop's, which Todd had refinished and used as his own, he pulled open a drawer where he'd kept a picture of his grandfather, with white hair and glasses, taken just before he died at sixty-one.

He showed the picture to Colton. "This is how I remember Pop," he said.

Colton stood holding the photo with both hands.[51] His head moved slowly left and right.

"Nobody's old in heaven," he said, handing the picture back

to his father. Leaving the room, he added, "And nobody wears glasses . . . you're like in your twenties and thirties."[52]

That prompted Todd to call his mother and ask her to send several pictures of her dad, Pop, at different ages.

A week or two later a manila envelope arrived. Todd pulled out a picture of Pop that was taken at the age of twenty-nine. As he and Sonja sat in the front room, Todd held up the photo for Colton to see. "What do you think of this?"

"Hey. How'd you get a picture of Pop?"[53] the boy said, casually moving on to play.

One of Sonja's most startling moments occurred one evening while she sat on the couch sorting through bills. Colton came up to her with a sense of purpose.

"Mommy, I've got two sisters."

"No, you have your sister, Cassie . . . do you mean your cousin Traci?"[54]

He shook his head. "You had a baby that died in your tummy."[55]

Time seemed to stop. Sonja's mouth dropped slightly as she looked directly at her son.

"How do you know you have two sisters,"[56] said Sonja in measured words, her mind racing, certain that her miscarriage two months into pregnancy—the most painful event of her life—was a topic she and Todd had *never* shared with their child. After all, she thought, *How do you explain to a four-year-old that a baby had died in your tummy.*

"*She* told me. And, she didn't have a name."[57]

Sonja could hear the clock ticking; the household was suddenly silent.

Responding to his mother's surprised look, Colton looked at her reassuringly. "It's okay, Mommy. God adopted her."[58]

Our baby was a girl? thought Sonja, unable to speak.

"She looked a lot like Cassie but she has dark hair. She kept hugging me. I didn't really like that."[59]

Sonja's eyes blinked rapidly as her little boy made one more startling statement: "She's just waiting for you to come to Heaven."[60]

Sonja pressed her lips together tightly, trying to swallow the lump that had begun to form in her throat.

What did Jesus look like? That was a question percolating in the minds of Todd and Sonja. Over the course of several months, they showed Colton multiple images and artistic renderings of Christ. Their son always shook his head. That wasn't the Jesus *he* met.

About three years after Colton's extraordinary experience in heaven, Todd was told about a news story that had appeared on CNN. It featured a young girl from Idaho, Akiane Kramarik, who had begun having visions of heaven at the age of four. Her descriptions were remarkably like Colton's.

At his computer Todd was able to download the CNN story from the archives. He watched it intently.

"Akiane," said the male voice-over, "is a self-taught artist who says her inspiration comes from above."[61] He went on to say that she began painting at the age of six.

Akiane herself, then twelve, came on camera to describe her vivid images of heaven.

"All the colors were out of this world. There are hundreds of millions of colors we don't know yet."

Then the CNN reporter's words caused Todd to physically move closer to the computer.

"Akiane describes God as vividly as she paints him," continued the narrator.

A remarkably compelling portrait of Jesus was filling the screen.

Back on camera the young girl spoke for herself. "He's pure. He's very masculine, really strong, and big. And his eyes are just beautiful."

Todd's memory instantly transported him to that moment when Colton had also said, "His eyes are soooo pretty."[62]

Quickly Todd extended his hand to press the computer space bar, freezing the picture on the screen.

"Colton!" he shouted to his now seven-year-old son. "Can you come here for a minute?"

His boy bounded into the room. "Yeah, Dad?"

Remembering how every image of Christ that he had previously passed in front of his son had failed to match Colton's recollection of Jesus, Todd pointed to the screen and said, "What's wrong with this one?"

Expressionlessly Colton stared at the screen. He glanced at his father.

"Dad, that one's right."[63]

Take a moment. Digest those thoughts: the testimony of two little four-year-old kids who never met . . . one who was either clinically dead or close to it . . . Colton, and another who had remarkable visions of God and heaven, Akiane, despite her family's atheistic beliefs . . . reported very similar images of heaven and Jesus . . . including the color of his eyes . . . and both agreed that the image of Christ that Akiane painted depicted Him, just as they remembered Him.

Later on, Colton provided an observation that seemed remarkably mature and encouraging. "You feel safe once you're in Heaven, because, you feel scared down here—what's going to happen and how are we going to survive—but, up there, you just feel safe."[64]

Moreover, says Colton, "I learned that heaven is for real and you're going to like it."[65]

Now, let's add one more innocent child's perspective of heaven. The experience of a six-year-old Alex who presumably died and came back to life.

ALEX, BACK FROM HEAVEN

As he pulled into the unfamiliar intersection, Kevin's mind tried to deal with three things at once.

A call to his wife, Beth.

"We're on our way home . . ."

Assessing whether there was any oncoming traffic . . .

And listening to his six-year-old son, Alex, strapped in his car seat in the back.

"Dad, I'm hungry."

Later recalling the snapshot in his mind—at an intersection he had never before taken—Kevin says, "I looked to the right, then to the left. But I didn't know that I was not looking down a perfectly straight half-mile stretch of road. Several hundred yards ahead was a huge dip that obscured anything that might have been there. The straight, empty road was a deadly optical illusion."

He wishes the next recollection was of something that never really happened.

"The deafening crunch of metal ripping metal flashed and then faded into brilliant silence. All was silence."

"I thought the accident was my fault," says Alex, from a little boy's perspective, "because I asked Daddy a question and he turned to answer my question right before the car hit us."

Thinking the roof of the car was going to collapse on him, Alex had tried to speak.

"I tried to call out to Daddy, but I couldn't hear the sound of my voice . . . with my lips I said, 'I love you, Daddy.'"

"I heard the sound of glass breaking and I saw Daddy's feet going out of the car. Then I saw something cool . . . five angels were carrying Daddy outside the car."[66]

He adds, "I'm not sure whether I watched Daddy from the car or from Heaven. I went to Heaven after the car hit us."

The force of the impact wrenched Kevin from the car and flung him into a ditch, where he lay unconscious for undetermined minutes.

Hearing the crash, a neighbor, former fireman Dan Tullis, rushed to the scene. He climbed into the backseat of the wrecked car, placing his hand over Alex's chest. There was no perceptible breathing. He pulled himself from the car and began to pray.

Another neighbor, Chris Leasure, was working in his front yard. He heard brakes squealing and the cacophony of a wreck.

"I took off running toward the accident," says Chris. "When I got in the backseat with Alex, his head was hanging down and he couldn't get air. I saw him take his last breath. I watched his body shudder and almost relax . . . I just felt he was passing . . . he was going to Heaven."[67]

In a daze, Kevin pulled himself from the ditch, stood, looked around, and ran to the car. Blood was running from a gash in Alex's forehead and his head seemed to be hanging unnaturally lower.

Alex felt an inexplicable peace: "Jesus came and got me from the car and kept me close to Him . . . I was above my body, watching everyone work on me. I was safe. Jesus kept talking to me, telling me I was going to be okay, so I was never afraid."[68]

Alex remembers, "I saw Daddy yelling my name, 'Alex, Alex, Alex!' Daddy didn't know where I was, and he was worried about me. A fireman put something in my mouth to help me breathe. They cut my shirt off. It was my plaid shirt."

Inside Kevin's mind, words were screaming: *Alex, my son . . . he looks dead! I've killed my son.*

Confirming those fears—his worst fears—he heard the heart-crushing statement of a first responder.

"We'll need to contact the coroner's office and cancel Med-Flight," said the first responder.[69]

Kevin, a trained psychotherapist, knew he was hearing that his son had died.

Then a policeman spoke: "But the chopper's already landing."

Dave Knopp, a paramedic dressed in the blue uniform of the MedFlight team, quickly assessed that Alex's pupils were fixed—unresponsive to light—and he wasn't breathing on his own.

"It was difficult to feel his pulse," says Dave, "but, I felt in my heart that we needed to pray."

He turned to Kevin, asking permission to pray for his son.

Kevin nodded yes.

"Once in the helicopter," remembers Dave, "I quickly laid my hand on Alex's head and prayed that he would be healed."

Alex—from above—recalls seeing Dave: "I saw the helicopter man bend over me and pray for me . . . I was not breathing. But Jesus said, 'You shouldn't worry. You are going to breathe again.' There were angels there too."[70]

Kevin recalls the terrible feeling of helplessness. "Tears streamed down my face as the doors of the chopper slammed shut. Will I ever see my little boy alive again? I had to get to Children's Hospital immediately."[71]

Alex's mom, Beth, arriving at the Columbus, Ohio, Nationwide Children's Hospital, spotted a blue-uniformed MedFlight paramedic in the parking lot: "I have a six-year-old son who just arrived by helicopter. Were you on the flight?"

"Yes, ma'am. My name's Dave Knopp."

"How bad is he?"

Something inside Dave caused him to be filled with a sudden boldness.

"Are you Christian?" he asked.

She nodded.

"Then listen to me. You're going to go into a trauma room . . . they're going to tell you your son is going to die . . . but I'm telling you . . . he's not going to die."[72]

"In the hospital I was watching everything from the corner of the emergency room, near the ceiling," says Alex. "Jesus was standing beside me . . . I was kind of blue . . . the doctors talked and they didn't have much good to say . . . they all thought I wouldn't make it. Jesus said I would."[73]

Then, as Alex saw doctors starting to put something down his throat, he says that Jesus moved him into heaven.

Alex vividly remembers what happened next.

"I went through a long, white tunnel that was very bright. I didn't like the music in the tunnel . . . but then, I got to Heaven and there was music and I loved it. The same five angels who helped Daddy out of the car were there. They comforted me."[74]

Only a "teaser" to what he would describe later, Alex says, "I saw pure white angels with fantastic wings who were all calling my name. They all said, 'Alex, go back.' I did go, but Jesus went with me and held me during my time in the emergency room."

In a recovery room, at his bedside, Kevin gazed upon his son, surrounded by monitors, wires, tubes, and medical paraphernalia, while a ventilator pumped air into his lungs.

Filled with fear, he pleaded for God to save his boy's life.

"God please forgive me for what I've done. Please protect him. Comfort him. I give you my son. I let go of him. He is yours. Please help him from the top of his head to the bottom of his feet."

"At the end of that prayer," says Kevin, "my spirit was bathed in a new sense of calm."[75]

Word got out, traveling thorough the neighborhoods of Columbus, about Alex, the little six-year-old boy who was struggling to hold on to a thread of life. People felt God tugging at their hearts to come to the hospital—some driving several hours. Soon every square inch of Alex's room was papered over with notes and prayers.[76]

Alex's grandfather, Dr. William Malarkey, a physician at Ohio State University, took Kevin through the X-rays and helped him understand the extraordinary degree of his son's injuries.[77]

"He suffered what is called internal decapitation," recalls Kevin. "For all intents and purposes, his head was not attached to his body. His spinal cord was severed."[78]

Further, he suffered "a broken pelvis, and traumatic brain injury. The injury to his spinal cord at the C1-C2 cervical vertebrae level—was so high that the spinal cord and brain constituted one massive injury field. That in itself is generally enough to cause death," reports Kevin.[79]

One of Alex's medical specialists was Dr. Raymond Onders, who had also treated actor Christopher Reeve for spinal-cord injury. He summarizes Alex's injuries:

"The vertebrae were completely detached. The tendon sheath around the spinal column was severed near the base of his brain. The injury was so severe and so high on the spinal column, it is simply incredible that Alex survived."

Kevin, Beth, and the growing community of supporters maintained a constant prayer vigil. "We prayed for Alex's brain, for his breathing, for the healing of his spine, and that the doorway to death would be locked shut for him," says Kevin.

One day, as Kevin and Beth prayed over their son, something changed: "Alex's lips formed into a slight but unmistakable smile. We looked at each other to confirm that we hadn't imagined it."

Tears of joy formed in their eyes.

"God was so good to give us this little encouraging sign . . . six weeks after the accident," says Kevin.[80]

The doctors told them that without surgical intervention his neck would never be stable.

Everyone continued to pray.

Then they received stunning news; the doctors concluded that the vertebrae had healed well without medical intervention.

"We're not sure what happened," said Alex's neurosurgeon, "but, we don't have to do the surgery."[81]

Little by little Alex made progress. His smiles became more frequent. He learned to communicate by moving his eyes and his mouth, answering yes or no. Finally, he could form words, then sentences.

"Today he is quadriplegic," explains Kevin, "immobile beneath his neck. He breathes on a ventilator, drives his wheelchair with his chin, and he surfs the Internet with a mouse he uses with his mouth."[82]

Alex couldn't wait to emerge from two months in a coma. He had so much to say about the things he'd experienced. Angels played a significant role in Alex's story, both in heaven and here on earth—at the scene of the accident and during his recovery in the hospital.

He remembers one particular day: "I saw angels in my room. They were everywhere. That made me have a really huge smile. There were so many of them I was a little scared. Daddy had never seen me smile like that," he says.

"Then the angels started to help me breathe . . . and put their hands on my chest to help me talk. I started to try to make words with my mouth and all of a sudden, I said 'Mom.' I tried to form the word 'Daddy' but it wouldn't come out."

He describes the angels.

"Angels aren't boys or girls. They are neither. They are completely white and they have wings."[83]

Alex says the angels talked to him, and encouraged him. Moreover, they had different jobs.[84]

"One made me feel better . . . another helped me open my mouth and make words . . . helping me breathe. Even when I couldn't talk, they could hear me."[85]

"When he came out of the coma," says Kevin, "he began talking about these extraordinary things . . . he wasn't excited, he wasn't scared, he talked about them the same way he talked about anything else."[86]

As a trained psychotherapist, Kevin questioned, *Were these "things" real or, because of the trauma, was his son simply hallucinating?*

"If anyone said they were skeptical," says Kevin, "I'd answer, 'I bet you weren't half as skeptical as I was.'"[87]

But finally, he came to fully believe his son, and the remarkable things that he described. "Alex has total recall of everything that occurred during the accident and total recall of everything that happened in Heaven."[88]

"When I went to Heaven," says Alex, "I arrived on the inside of the gate . . . other people who came to Heaven were all on the outside of the gate. The gate is really tall, and it's white, very shiny, and looks like it has scales like a fish."[89]

Alex explains his sense that there was a distinct "inner and outer" aspect to heaven. He arrived at an "inner Heaven . . . where everything is brighter and more intense.

"I went through a light and I heard music," remembers Alex, "there were colors. Then I was in the presence of God. He had a body that was like a human body, but it was a lot bigger. I could only see up to His neck. He had on a white robe that was very bright. I looked down at my legs, I could move them again. Everything was perfect.

"I didn't see any people," he continues, "only God, Jesus, and angels.[90] As they do their jobs the angels make beautiful songs for God. Some are messengers, some are warriors, and some are worshippers."[91]

Music made an impact upon him. "The music is beautiful . . . nothing like the music here. It is perfect. Perfect is my favorite word for describing Heaven."[92] As the six-year-old was given back his life and returned to earth, he felt he was given a mission.

"I know I'm supposed to share some of what I have seen in Heaven . . . God has told me not to tell about other things. I know I'm with God when I am visiting Heaven, but you can't see God on His throne . . . the angels fly so fast that they block Him from view. Nobody gets to see God's face until later."[93]

"Heaven is not the next world, it is now . . . not up in the sky . . . it is everywhere and nowhere. Heaven is a place that is not a place. Heaven is a time with no past, present or future, it is always now."[94]

Alex adds a statement we've heard from others, including Don Piper and Colton Burpo: "Heaven is real. The whole Heaven place is real."

He made one other observation that leaves us thinking: "There is a hole in outer Heaven. That hole goes to Hell."

POSTSCRIPT TO ALEX'S STORY

One Sunday morning Kevin Malarkey was driving home from church with his younger boy, Aaron. He'd promised him an ice-cream cone.

The man behind the counter at Dairy Queen looked curiously at Kevin.

"You don't remember me, do you?" said the man, extending his hand.

"My name is Chris Leasure. I was at the accident scene . . . with your son. I prayed for him to be all right."

"That's incredible. You were there?"

"Yes."

Kevin looked at him, amazed at the Divine Alignment of God.

That stop at Dairy Queen was an impromptu decision, and here he was meeting a person who had been Divinely Aligned to play a role in the unfolding of Alex's extraordinary story. He now knew, of course, that prayer from people like Chris played a critical role in Alex's survival.

"From a human perspective, life is random, and sometimes random turns out well," reasons Kevin. "But I know God put Chris directly in my path that Sunday."[95]

The remarkable story of Alex Malarkey, told through his father, Kevin, is relived in a bestseller called *The Boy Who Came Back from Heaven*.

WHAT CAN WE MAKE OF ALL THIS?

It's one thing for us to doubt the stories of adults who tell us they have had similar experiences in visiting and returning from heaven, but two four-year-olds and a six-year-old? Who lived miles apart? Who had never met?

Let's take another look at that list of fifteen similar experiences I've compiled that Dr. Robert Moody and others say we should expect when we go to heaven, now converted to a chart, compared to the expectations of the Bible.

Listed are the salient comments and descriptions of heaven from Dr. Moody's 150 patients plus the reports of the 6 persons in this book. The columns identify which persons had which experiences: Dr. Moody's patients (Dr. M); Don Piper (DP); Nathan Christensen (NC); and Cynthia Farrington (CF); then the three children, Akiane Kramarik (AK), Colton Burpo (CB), and Alex Malarkey (AM). Finally, our list of similarities is compared with what we've been told to expect in the Bible (B).

CHART OF SIMILARITIES OF HEAVEN

	DR. M	DP	NC	CF	AK	CB	AM	B	
1. You are outside your physical body; perhaps in the same physical area; a spectator of yourself.	✓					✓	✓		
2. You enter darkness, feeling rapid movement through a tunnel, approaching a distant light and warmth.	✓	✓		✓			✓		
3. You may notice you have a new body that is different, yet perfect; there's an absence of pain or fear	✓	✓		✓			✓	✓	Cor. 15: 42–44 Rev. 21:5 Rom. 8:18
4. A loving being of light greets you, perhaps nonverbally; and/or a strong feeling of love, joy, and peace replace sorrow.	✓	✓		✓			✓	✓	Rev. 21:4
5. It is never dark in heaven; brilliant lightness and whiteness is believed to come from God.		✓	✓	✓	✓	✓	✓	✓	Rev. 21: 23–25
6. You will be greeted by friends and relatives who have been restored to look their best.	✓	✓		✓		✓	✓	✓	Rev. 21:5

	DR.M	DP	NC	CF	AK	CB	AM	B	
7. There are borders, a gate described as "pearly" and like "fish scales," and golden streets.	✓	✓					✓	✓	Rev. 21: 12–21
8. You hear intense, extraordinary music, singing—perhaps several compositions all at once.		✓		✓			✓	✓	Rev. 14:2
9. There are bright, indescribable colors.		✓			✓	✓	✓		
10. There are multiple angels with white wings.		✓				✓	✓	✓	Matt. 10:10
11. You may encounter God, whose face is not visible and/or Jesus, with beautiful eyes.			✓		✓	✓	✓		
12. You may be told to return, it's not your time; but may prefer to stay because of the love and joy.	✓	✓		✓		✓	✓		
13. On earth you avoid telling others; or, it's hard to describe and you don't think they'll believe you, yet you are no longer afraid to die.	✓	✓		✓			✓		

	DR.M	DP	NC	CF	AK	CB	AM	B	
14. You learn that prayers of people on earth—sometimes many people—have had an effect upon your return from heaven.		✓	✓			✓	✓		
15. You are no longer afraid to die.	✓	✓		✓					

THERE IS MUCH TO BE SAID FOR HEAVEN

Our collection of commonalities by eyewitnesses of heaven provides a compelling picture of what we may find. Still, my spiritual guide Jeff Winter acknowledges the degree of difficulty it must be to describe what one has seen in heaven.

"It would be like twins inside their mother's womb. One twin comes out and tries to explain to his sibling, still inside the womb, what it's like here on the outside."

Indeed.

Yet, doubts will linger for many among us. As persuasive as these reports are, it's our human nature to be skeptical. After all, one could argue that Don Piper experienced things that, as a pastor himself, he would have expected to find in heaven simply by studying his Bible. Could it be that his trip to heaven was merely a subconscious event? Perhaps an hallucination?

Nathan is a pastor's son. While in a coma, did he merely imagine what he'd been led to expect about afterlife from his dad? Same for four-year-old Colton, also a pastor's son?

Of course, each has also told things that they witnessed, which are not written in the scriptures. And there are others among Dr.

Moody's patients and within this book who had no biblical schooling prior to giving their reports.

In the end, you will come to your own decision as to the credibility of the foregoing stories.

HOW ABOUT HELL?

Jeff Winter says that, perhaps not surprisingly, hell has much less to be said for it than heaven.

The Bible talks less about hell than heaven; it is mentioned 54 times[96] vs. 551 for heaven.[97] In fact, only in a parable told by Jesus is hell described to any degree.

You may remember that story, about a nameless rich man and Lazarus.

The wealthy man often passed a beggar at the gate of his elegant home. We later learn that the beggar's name was Lazarus, and that he died and went to heaven, finding himself next to Abraham, the patriarch from whom all Jews and Christians trace their descent.

About the same time as Lazarus, the rich man also died. But he went to hell, or Hades.

"In Hades," says the Bible, "he was in torment."

Looking up, the rich man could see Abraham with Lazarus by his side.

"Have pity on me," cried out the rich man. "Send Lazarus with a drop of water for my tongue—I am in agony in this fire."

Abraham reminded the rich man that in his lifetime he had received good things—probably by living on the dark side, choosing to cheat others—while suggesting that Lazarus was poor on earth, yet lived in the goodness of light.

"Besides," said Abraham, "a great chasm has been set in place so that those who want to go from here to you, cannot. Nor can anyone crossover from there to us."

Accepting that rationale, the rich man then cried out to Abraham, requesting that he send Lazarus back to earth from heaven so he could warn the rich man's brothers—"so they won't come to this place of torment."

Abraham explained that the people of earth had already been told by Moses and the prophets . . . including Jesus Himself . . . therefore, "Let them listen to them."

The rich man argued that if his brothers could hear it directly from someone who had *been* in heaven—Lazarus—they would hear sufficient testimony to feel remorse and repent for their ways of living on the dark side.

"If they do not listen to Moses and the Prophets," said Abraham with finality, "they will not be convinced even if someone rises from the dead."[98]

In other words, even if Lazarus returned from heaven to tell everyone what he saw, the folks would still have doubts.

While the stories of several witnesses of heaven are revealed in this book, there is no comparably long list of witnesses who have returned from hell to tell us about their experiences there.

"What the Bible tells us about hell," summarizes Jeff Winter, "is that it's a place of anguish and torment. It's hot—there's an unquenchable fire. And, according to Jesus, it's a place where there is weeping and gnashing of teeth."[99]

THE CHOICE AT THE JUNCTION

Some will linger as they travel along their track through life.

There are many temptations to remain on the dark rail. To hold yourself in the shadows. To allow secrets to keep you in darkness. Thinking that as long as you are not in the light, your noncommitment will go unnoticed. Thinking that choosing to travel by light would mean you need to give up stuff that you are clinging to—things you know are wrong, full of resentment, or secrets.

But, in the end, your track will end. Your junction will appear. There'll be no more indecision. Time's up. The choice will be yours. Light or dark. Heaven or hell.

HOW DO I CHOOSE THE PATH TO HEAVEN?

How to *get* to heaven is an age-old question, and, perhaps, one of the most complicated of all.

For those who have studied and understood the Christian Bible, there is little question how you get your ticket to heaven: "Jesus answered, 'I am the way and the truth and the life. No one comes to the Father except through me.'"[100]

But, you might ask, what about everyone else? What about those of a different faith? Or those who, through no fault of their own, such as in third-world countries, never learned the teachings of the Bible? What about babies who die before they can speak?

C. S. Lewis was puzzled by the same questions.

"Is it not frightfully unfair that this new life (in Heaven) should be confined to people who have heard of Christ and been able to believe in Him?" he asked.

He then offered: "But the truth is, God has not told us what His arrangements about the other people are.

"We *do* know that no man can be saved except through Christ; we do *not* know that *only those who know Him* can be saved through Him."[101]

> The intention of the Holy Spirit is to teach us
> how one goes to heaven, not how the heavens go.
>
> GALILEO[102]

CONCLUSION

If you've yet to decide, I can tell you that there is considerable data confirming that people who live their lives in the light—basically following the rules that are written in the Ten Commandments—have happier and healthier lives than those who remain on the dark rail.

AMAZING DATA IN SUPPORT OF FAITH

Recently, two doctors in England evaluated an extraordinary number of research studies on whether there is a link between faith and health—twelve hundred studies and four hundred reviews in all. The results were impressive. They concluded that 81 percent of the studies showed benefit and only 4 percent harm, the latter primarily including persons who avoided medical attention on religious grounds.

Alex Bunn and David Randall reported that one of those studies followed over twenty-one thousand American adults more than a nine-year period. They summarized: "Those who attended church regularly had a life expectancy seven years longer than those who did not. For black people the benefit was fourteen years."

Believing in God and living in the light, as opposed to the dark, was also cited as a cause of better mental health.

Overall, the majority of studies correlated faith with the following beneficial outcomes:

- Well-being, happiness, and life satisfaction
- Hope and optimism
- Purpose and meaning in life
- Higher self-esteem
- Better adaptation to bereavement
- Greater social support and less loneliness
- Lower rates of depression and faster recovery from depression
- Lower rates of suicide and fewer positive attitudes toward suicide
- Less anxiety; less psychosis and fewer psychotic tendencies
- Lower rates of alcohol and drug abuse
- Less delinquency and criminal activity
- Greater marital stability and satisfaction

If you could extend your lifetime by seven to fourteen years, as Bunn and Randall suggest, and enjoy all of the foregoing benefits, isn't it worth thinking about traveling through life on the light rail . . . instead of the dark one?

SCIENCE VS. GOD

As I said early on in this book, I'm not a doctor, a philosopher, or a theologian. Those folks are much more learned than humble me, a mere author and TV guy—*Schoolhouse Rock!* founder—who specializes in simplicity.

It is my role to *study* what smart people say, then report it.

One of those is Lee Strobel, former atheist, law reporter, and now bestselling author of such persuasive books as *The Case for a Creator*. Lee has done all the painstaking work of researching what many other very smart persons have said about the existence of God in a world where atheistic scientists have sometimes tried to sound like they themselves were God.

Strobel, a zealot for science in high school, read what was proffered about evolution and Darwin and became a devout atheist. Later, his legal and journalistic training was challenged when his wife became a believer and churchgoer.

That caused him "to investigate what was going on." Subsequently he said, "I began asking questions about faith, God and the Bible . . . determined to go wherever the answers would take me . . . though, frankly, I wasn't quite prepared for where I would ultimately end up."[1]

He became a believer. As well, one of the most articulate defenders of God in a world where the mass media and the universities seem to be in collusion to cover up the evidence that Lee Strobel and others have found to make a case for God.

I'd like to share some morsels of that evidence here, excerpting from Lee Strobel's book, in which he lays out his case like a meticulous litigator.

GOD OR NO GOD?

On this question Lee interviewed a scholar who has written more than fifty articles on science and faith, Talbot School of Theology professor J. P. Moreland, who says, "You can't get something from nothing. If the universe began with dead matter, how, then, do you get something totally different—consciousness, living, thinking, feeling, believing creatures—from materials that don't have that?"[2]

At Messiah College, Lee interviewed professor Robin Collins, author of such books as *A Scientific Argument for the Existence of God*.

Professor Collins contends that we live in a universe "that has just the right conditions to sustain life. The coincidences are simply too amazing to have been the result of happenstance . . . the impression of design is overwhelming."[3]

In England, Lee spoke with Alister McGrath, of Oxford, who said, "The truth claims of atheism simply cannot be proved." Moreover, "The simple fact of the matter is that atheism is a faith, which draws conclusions that go beyond the available evidence."[4]

THE BEGINNING OF TIME

Most debates on the question of "Is there a God or no God?" end up at the beginning of time. Nearly all scientists agree that the universe began over fourteen billion years ago with what they describe as a single Big Bang.

Believers quote the Bible: "In the beginning God created the heavens and the earth . . . and God said, 'Let there be light,' and there was light."[5]

Meanwhile nonbelieving scientists say, well, they don't know how the Big Bang happened, but they are convinced that one day they will have concrete evidence to deny the biblical claim that God created the universe.

Lee Strobel traveled to Spokane to meet with Stephen Meyer, PhD, an associate professor of philosophy at Whitmore College and one of the leading voices on science and intelligent design.

Professor Meyer made this astonishing argument for the perfection of God's universe: "The expansion rate of the universe is fine-tuned to one part in a trillion, trillion, trillion, trillion, trillion. If it were changed by one part in either direction—a little faster, a little slower—we could not have a universe that would be capable of supporting life."

His conclusion: "What we know today gives us heightened confidence—from science—that God exists."

Professor Meyer adds a postscript: "I think of the wry smile that might be on the lips of God as . . . evidence for the reliability of the Bible and for His creation of the universe; I believe He . . . delights when we discover His fingerprints in the vastness of the universe, in the dusty relics of paleontology and in the complexity of the cell."[6]

Like a courtroom attorney making his final argument, Lee Strobel sums up the evidence on God's side in the debate over creation of the universe: "The cosmological constant, which represents the energy density of space, is as precise as throwing a dart from space and hitting a bull's-eye just a trillionth of a trillionth of an inch in diameter on Earth."[7]

SUMMING UP

I am hopeful that these pages have presented you with a modicum of evidence that there is much benefit to be derived in choosing to travel through the remainder of your lifetime by stepping from the shadows into the light. For, in this action, I believe that you, like Darryl Strawberry and others who have testified in this book, will discover that your life will be immensely better, your hopes will be higher, and love will last you forever.

If you think that's the case, then go ahead: follow the Seven Steps that lead you to the discovery of the full potential of your own personal GPS—God's Positioning System.

GPS STEP 1: SPEAK WITH THE NAVIGATOR
Program your GPS. Engage in out-loud or silent communication, multiple times a day. Pray.

GPS STEP 2: LISTEN TO YOUR INNER COMPASS
Each of us has a God-installed compass; a "still small voice" within. Tuning in to and listening to your inner compass is often the most important directive we can follow.

GPS STEP 3: MAP YOUR DESTINATION

Determine the direction you believe your destiny is taking you. Write it down. Make choices to travel in the light, not darkness. Go.

GPS STEP 4: UNSHACKLE YOUR BAGGAGE

Learn to unshackle yourself from hurtful habits, resentment, and guilt—cutting you free to allow God to propel you more quickly to your destination.

GPS STEP 5: STEP OUT IN FAITH AND BELIEVE YOU'LL ARRIVE

Your destiny will not come to you. You need to continually talk with your Navigator, programming your GPS, then step out in faith. Your highway to Providence will continue to unfold, even on the most uncertain days, regardless of the twists and turns you encounter.

GPS STEP 6: READ THE SIGNS, RECALCULATE, AND ACCELERATE

Godwinks are the reassuring signposts along your path, letting you know you're going in the right direction. Watch for "danger" signs and recalculate from time to time by reprogramming your GPS— God's Positioning System. Once on track, put your foot on the accelerator!

GPS STEP 7: GRATEFULLY ARRIVE WITH A FULL WELL WITHIN

Once you fill the wonderful Well Within with God's love, you'll reach destinations in accord with God's purpose for you. Express gratitude for your arrival, and ask your GPS Navigator what He wants you to do next.

FINALLY, COME TO TERMS WITH YOUR OWN ULTIMATE ARRIVAL: GETTING TO HEAVEN

How do you do that? Study the ancient scriptures; talk with faith counselors; and revisit the opinions on "How to Get to Heaven" at the end of the last chapter.

A FINAL MESSAGE FROM A RE-INVENTOR

In Chapter 6, I told the story of Steven Jobs, who went from the boy-wonder inventor of the Macintosh computer to the man whose company was taken from him, and how, from the ashes of being fired, he built two more successful companies before returning to lead Apple into an era of unbelievable growth, becoming the most valuable company in the world.[8]

When he died young, at fifty-six, of cancer, many wished to know: did he believe in God?

By reading his biography, we learn that Steve continually questioned the existence of God, but according to author Walter Isaacson, "Steve wanted to believe in an afterlife."[9]

Yet, an extraordinary insight about the last moments of Steven Jobs came from a eulogy given by his sister, Mona Simpson. Let me share it in this final story.

STEVE'S ENTHUSIASTIC DEPARTURE

Steven Jobs represented many things to youthful dreamers.

He was a visionary who could visualize the perfect outcome for a product or company, and was a legendary taskmaster in achieving that vision.

He also maintained a youthful excitement. One can imagine the always blue-jean clad Steve expressing a joyous passion for each new creation, from his first Macintosh to his first iPhone or iPad—and after all his hard work, gazing upon something truly beautiful, gasping "wow" with enthusiasm.

Still, one wonders, did Steve believe in God when he reached the final junction of his railroad track through life?

Mona Simpson, Steve's sister, provided that insight with her eulogy at the small family funeral.

She told how her brother, who had been put up for adoption at birth, had sought her out when she was twenty-five—he was about twenty-nine. She describes their first meeting.

"We took a long walk. He felt like someone I'd pick to be a friend." Yet, it was more than that, she says: "My whole life I'd been waiting for a man to love, who could love me . . . I met that man and he was my brother."

The more they got to know each other, the deeper their bond grew. She remembers the day he enthusiastically phoned to say, "There's this beautiful woman and she's really smart and she has this dog and I'm going to marry her."

Later on he was a doting father, worried about his daughter's boyfriends, and always maintained a priority for his family.

"Even as a young millionaire," she recalls, "Steve always picked me up at the airport. He'd be standing there in his jeans." When one of his children called him at work, his secretary would say, "Your dad's in a meeting. Would you like me to interrupt him?"

He was humble, loved to keep learning, "and," says Mona, "Steve had a lot of fun. He treasured happiness.

"What I learned from my brother's death," she continues, "was that character is essential: What he was, was how he died."

Mona takes us through the final hours of her brother's life.

"He called me to ask me to hurry up to Palo Alto. His tone was affectionate, dear, loving, but like someone whose luggage was already strapped onto the vehicle, who was already on the beginning of his journey, even as he was sorry, truly deeply sorry, to be leaving us.

"He started his farewell and I stopped him. I said, 'Wait. I'm coming. I'm in a taxi to the airport. I'll be there.'

"He said: 'I'm telling you now because I'm afraid you won't make it on time, honey.'

"When I arrived, he and his Laurene were joking together like partners who'd lived and worked together every day of their lives. He looked into his children's eyes as if he couldn't unlock his gaze."

Mona says that contrary to doctors' expectations, he did continue holding on a bit longer. "Then, after a while, it was clear that he would no longer wake to us. His breathing changed. It became severe, deliberate, purposeful."

Steve spoke to his sister. "He told me, when he was saying goodbye and telling me he was sorry, so sorry we wouldn't be able to be old together as we'd always planned, that he was going to a better place."

This says something that should be underscored. Steven Jobs felt he was going to a *better place*.

Mona then says, "Before embarking, he looked for a long time at his children, then at his life's partner, Laurene, and then over their shoulders past them."

In a final expression of genuine enthusiasm—upon seeing something even greater than any Apple product he might have held in his lap—Steve Jobs spoke his last words:

"Oh, wow. Oh, wow. Oh, wow!"[10]

What did he see—as he looked into the distance? Was he seeing angels or the lights of heaven beckoning him? There's only one way for you to ever know. To choose the path to heaven yourself; and when you get there, sit down and have a chat with him.

FINAL WORD

Thanks for taking this journey with me. I hope you'll report back your stories of triumph as you program your own GPS—constantly talking with the Navigator, listening to your inner compass, un-shackling yourself from your baggage, and arriving at your earthy destinations with a full, and contented, Well Within.

Let me know if you've moved from the rail in the shadows to the one in light. I'd love to hear your godwink stories of freedom and accomplishment. Write facebook.com/godwinks, or squire@whengodwinks.com.

And remember, if at any point in your journey you feel that your GPS is unclear or uncertain, always go back to Step One: **Talk to the Navigator.**

ACKNOWLEDGMENTS

T o tell you the truth, I don't feel as though I actually write my own books—I just write them down. The credit goes to God.

Of course, there are many who deserve acknowledgment in helping to birth this book.

The lineup includes my literary agents, Jennifer Gates and Todd Shuster. What a team. Jennifer draws upon years of publishing house experience as an editor, anticipating a publisher's questions and concerns, while her partner Todd Shuster, a skilled and respected man of the law, provides pathways to stronger relationships.

Jonathan Merkh, an impressively visionary publisher, has once again placed me under the leadership of a top-rate team, this time led by editor-in-chief Becky Nesbitt and associate editor Amanda Demastus, who have firmly nurtured this book with vitality and grace.

Yet, not for a moment in any day, am I not counseled wisely and supported fully by my spiritual guide and 100 percent love-of-my-life-wife—Louise DuArt.

NOTES

CHAPTER ONE: SPEAK WITH THE NAVIGATOR

1. DeBakey reports in endnotes.
2. "Understanding Your Ejection Fraction," my.clevelandclinic.org/heart/ disorders/heartfailure/ejectionfraction.aspx, accessed December 30, 2011.
3. Rose Ybarra, *The Monitor*, December 26, 2004.
4. Photocopies of those comparative reports are found in the endnotes.
5. Anita Onarecker Wood, *Divine Appointment* (Brenham, TX: Lucid Books, 2010), 9.
6. Don Piper speech at First Chinese Baptist Church, Mountain Valley, CA, posted by faisoft, March 10, 2008; www.youtube.com/ watch?v=u8E2UAV_3w4, 50:20, accessed March 28, 2011.
7. Don Piper, *Heaven Is Real* (New York: Berkley Publishing, 2007), 12.
8. Ibid., 24.
9. "Beyond Belief," *Nightline*, abcnews.go.com/Nightline/video/don-pipers-90 -minutes-heaven-pastor-pronounced-dead-hears-music-beyond-spectacular -nightline-14227574; 2:37–2:57, accessed August 24, 2011.
10. Don Piper speech, Mountain Valley, CA; 47:25.
11. "Beyond Belief," *Nightline*, :13–:24.
12. Ibid., 2:13–2:22
13. Wood, *Divine Appointment*, 179.
14. Piper, *Heaven Is Real*, 203.
15. Wood, *Divine Appointment*, 177.

16. Dr. Tom Faciszewski, www.marshfieldclinic.org/patients/?page=provider details&ID=32556, Marshfield Clinic, 1000 N. Oak Avenue, Marshfield, Wisconsin, 54449.

17. "P.O.D.—Alive Lyrics," www.lyrics007.com/P.O.D.%20Lyrics/Alive%20 |Lyrics.html, accessed December 30, 2011.

CHAPTER TWO: LISTEN TO YOUR INNER COMPASS

1. 1 Kings 19:12 (KJV).

2. Francis Collins, *The Language of God* (New York: Simon & Schuster, 2006), 2.

3. Ibid., 3.

4. Ibid., 20.

5. Ibid., 23.

6. Ibid., 25.

7. Ibid., 29.

8. Ibid., 30.

9. Wernher von Braun, "My Faith," *American Weekly*, February 10, 1963.

10. Collins, *The Language of God*, 146.

11. 1 Kings 19:12 (NIV).

12. Ibid.

13. Leo Thorsness, *Surviving Hell* (New York: Encounter Books, 2008), 10.

14. Jane South Ellis, interview, September 28, 2010.

15. Irene Gut Opdyke, *In My Hands* (New York: Alfred A. Knopf, 1999), 117.

16. Ibid., 35.

17. Ibid., 95.

18. Ibid., 142–43.

19. Ibid., 157.

20. Ibid., 158.

21. Ibid., 166

22. Ibid., 201.

23. Jeannie Opdyke Smith, interview, April 23, 2009.

24. Ibid., 214.

25. Ibid., 215.

26. Opdyke, *In My Hands*, 214.

27. Ibid., 263.

28. Ibid., 267.

29. Steve Waldman, "Irena's Vow, Catholic Heroism, and God's Winks," blog .beliefnet.com/stevenwaldman/2009/03/irenas-vow-catholic-heroism-an .html, accessed January 3, 2012.

30. Dan Gordon, *Postcards from Heaven* (New York: Free Press; 2008), 70–71.
31. Ibid., 105.

CHAPTER THREE: MAPPING YOUR DESTINATION
1. Richard Ouzounian, "One Laugh Changed Carol Burnett's Life," *Toronto Star*, June 6, 2009, www.thestar.com/comment/columnists/article/645801, accessed January 3, 2012.
2. Carol Burnett, *One More Time* (New York: Random House, 1986), 186.
3. Ibid., 223.
4. Ibid.
5. Ibid., 272.
6. Ibid., 289–90.
7. Ibid., 292.
8. Andy Stanley, *The Principle of the Path* (Nashville: Thomas Nelson, 2009), 14.

CHAPTER FOUR: UNSHACKLE YOUR BAGGAGE
1. "Tyler Perry: Bio," www.tylerperry.com/biography/, accessed January 3, 2012.
2. "The Many Faces of Tyler Perry," interview, 700 Club, www.cbn.com/media/player/index.aspx?s=/vod/KW44, accessed January 3, 2012.
3. Ibid.
4. Ibid.
5. Ibid.
6. Carrie Fisher, "BrainyQuote: Carrie Fisher Quotes," www.brainyquote.com/quotes/authors/c/carrie_fisher.html, accessed January 3, 2012.
7. Anne Beiler, *Twist Of Faith* (Nashville; Thomas Nelson Publishers, 2008) 7.
8. Ibid., 17.
9. Ibid., 24.
10. Ibid., 23.
11. Ibid., 27.
12. Ibid., 29.
13. Ibid., 188.
14. Ibid., 192.
15. Ibid., 193.
16. Ibid., 199.
17. Ibid., 205.
18. Ibid., 206.
19. Ibid., 33.

20. Ibid., 47.
21. Ibid., 96.
22. Ibid., 75.
23. Ibid., 83.
24. Ibid., 88.
25. *The 700 Club*, CBN TV www.cbn.com/700club/guests/bios/Anne_Beiler_030408.aspx, accessed February 14, 2012.
26. "The Seven Baby Steps," www.daveramsey.com/new/baby-steps, accessed January 3, 2012.
27. "Pollyanna," Wikipedia, en.wikipedia.org/wiki/Pollyanna; accessed August 26, 2011.

CHAPTER FIVE: STEP OUT IN FAITH AND BELIEVE YOU'LL ARRIVE

1. Os Hillman, www.marketplaceleaders.org.
2. Os Hillman, *Today God Is First* (Ventura, CA: Regal Books, 2007), 369.

CHAPTER SIX: READ THE SIGNS, RECALCULATE, AND ACCELERATE

1. SQuire Rushnell, *When God Winks on New Beginnings* (Nashville: Thomas Nelson, 2009), 71–76.

CHAPTER SEVEN: GRATEFULLY ARRIVE WITH A FULL WELL WITHIN

1. Darryl Strawberry, *Straw* (New York: HarperCollins, 2009), 135.
2. Ibid., 21.
3. Ibid., 25.
4. Ibid., 26.
5. Ibid., 37.
6. Ibid., 39–41.
7. Ibid., 51.
8. Ibid., 60.
9. Ibid., 63.
10. Ibid., 64.
11. Ibid., 77.
12. Ibid., 78.
13. Ibid., 72.
14. Ibid., 74.

15. Ibid., 83.
16. Ibid., 101.
17. Ibid., 112.
18. Ibid., 113.
19. Ibid., 106.
20. Ibid., 85.
21. Ibid., 86.
22. Ibid., 121.
23. Ibid., 122.
24. Ibid., 122.
25. Ibid., 123.
26. Ibid., 125.
27. Ibid., 142.
28. Ibid., 143.
29. Ibid., 146.
30. Ibid., 158.
31. Ibid., 173.
32. Ibid., 175.
33. Ibid., 193.
34. Ibid., 197–98.
35. Ibid., 203.
36. Ibid., 213.
37. Ibid., xi, Introduction.

WHAT'S NEXT? THE ULTIMATE ARRIVAL

1. 1 Corinthians 2:9.
2. Luke 10:20.
3. Revelation 21:4.
4. Romans 8:18
5. Revelation 21:11–25.
6. Raymond A. Moody, Jr., *Life After Life* (Atlanta: Mockingbird Books, 1975), 18–19.
7. Don Piper speech at First Chinese Baptist Church, Mountain Valley, California, posted by faisoft, March 10, 2008, www.youtube.com/watch?v=u8E2UAV_3w4, 50:20, accessed January 4, 2012.
8. Akiane and Foreli Kramarik, *Akiane: Her Life, Her Art, Her Poetry* (Nashville: Thomas Nelson, 2006), 7.
9. Ibid., 12.

10. Ibid., 14.

11. Akiane Kramarik interview, www.youtube.com/watch?v=-YdIVeBo8SE, posted July 29, 2006, accessed January 4, 2012.

12. Akiane and Foreli Kramarik, *Akiane: Her Life, Her Art, Her Poetry*, 21.

13. Ibid., 26.

14. Ibid., 27.

15. Ibid., 28.

16. Akiane Kramarik interview, www.youtube.com/watch?rmm-0-Rdxo8#(1:00); 10/14/07; accessed 1/8/12.

17. Ibid., 1:50–2:02.

18. Ibid., 3:02–3:10.

19. Todd Burpo, *Heaven Is for Real*, (Nashville: Thomas Nelson, 2010).

20. Colton Burpo; *The 700 Club*, CBN TV, Carrie Matso, www.cbn.com/700club/features/amazing/iCM6_colton_burpo.aspx, accessed 12/17/11.

21. *700 Club*, Matso.

22. Burpo, *Heaven Is for Real*, 35.

23. *700 Club*, Matso.

24. Burpo, *Heaven Is for Real*, 43.

25. *700 Club*, Matso.

26. Burpo, *Heaven Is for Real*, 48.

27. Ibid., 51.

28. Ibid., xvii.

29. *700 Club*, Matso.

30. Burpo, *Heaven Is for Real*, xix.

31. Burpo, *Heaven Is for Real*, xx.

32. Todd Burpo; *Today* NBC, Kathie Lee Gifford (2:11), 3/21/11; http://today.msnbc.msn.com/id/42191453/ns/today-today_people/t/meet-boy-who-says-he-visited-heaven-saw-jesus#.TwjA-yPpAdk, accessed 12/17/11.

33. Burpo, *Heaven Is for Real*, xx.

34. Ibid., xx.

35. Ibid., 63.

36. Todd Burpo; *Today* NBC, Matt Lauer (3:26), 3/21/11; http://today.msnbc.msn.com/id/42191453/ns/today-today_people/t /meet-boy-who-says-he-visited-heaven-saw-jesus#.TwjA-yPpAdk, accessed 12/17/11.

37. Burpo, *Heaven Is for Real*, 64.

38. *700 Club*, Matso.

39. Burpo, *Heaven Is for Real*, 67.

40. Burpo, *Heaven Is for Real*, 68

41. Ibid., 79.

42. Ibid., 81.

43. Todd Burpo, *The 700 Club* CBN TV (6:02), March 21, 2011; www.cbn.com/media/player/index.aspx?s=/vod/iCM6v2_WS (6:02), accessed 1/13/12

44. *700 Club* TV (6:15).

45. *700 Club*, Matso.

46. Burpo, *Heaven Is for Real*, 86.

47. *700 Club* TV(4:37).

48. Burpo, *Heaven Is for Real*, 88.

49. *Today*, Lauer (1:38).

50. Burpo, *Heaven Is for Real*, 104.

51. Ibid., 121.

52. *Today*, Gifford (4:42).

53. Burpo, *Heaven Is for Real*, 122.

54. Ibid., 94.

55. *700 Club* TV (4:38).

56. *700 Club* TV (4:45).

57. *Today*, Gifford (2:50).

58. Burpo, *Heaven Is for Real*, 95.

59. *700 Club* TV (4:51).

60. *700 Club* TV (4:56).

61. CNN TV interview; www.youtube.com/watch?v=rmm-0-Rdxo8&feature=related (:22), accessed 12/17/11.

62. Burpo, *Heaven Is for Real*, 144.

63. Ibid., 145.

64. *Today*, Gifford (3:43).

65. *700 Club*, Matso.

66. Kevin and Alex Malarkey, *The Boy Who Came Back from Heaven*, (Carol Stream, IL: Tyndale House Publishers, 2010), 14.

67. Ibid., 152.

68. Ibid., 122–23.

69. Ibid., 9.

70. Ibid., 124.

71. Ibid., 18.

72. Ibid., 25–27.

73. Ibid., 30.

74. Ibid., 16.

75. Ibid., 41.

76. Ibid., 43.

77. "The Boy Who Came Back from Heaven," *Coast to Coast with George Noory*, ww.youtube.com/watch?v=OiYLVF53ZRQ, 4:35, accessed January 4, 2012.

78. Ibid., 1:17.

79. Malarkey, *The Boy Who Came Back from Heaven*, 59.

80. Ibid., 84.

81. Ibid., 92.

82. Noory, 2:20–2:30.

83. Malarkey, *The Boy Who Came Back from Heaven*, 86.

84. Ibid., 115.

85. Ibid., 87.

86. Noory, 4:10.

87. Ibid., 4:30.

88. Ibid., 5:45–5:59.

89. Malarkey, *The Boy Who Came Back from Heaven*, 49.

90. Ibid., 48.

91. Ibid., 87.

92. Ibid., 50.

93. Ibid., 191.

94. Ibid., 48.

95. Ibid., 152.

96. KJV; www.wiki.answers.com/Q/How_many_times_is_hell_mentioned_in_the_Bible.

97. KHJ; www.wiki.answers.com/Q/How_many_times_is_the_word_heaven_mentioned_in_the_Bible.

98. Luke 16:19–31.

99. Matt. 25:30.

100. John 14:6.

101. C. S. Lewis, *A Year With C. S. Lewis* (London: HarperCollins, 2003), 169.

102. en.wikiquote.org/wiki/Galileo_Galilei.

CONCLUSION.

1. Lee Strobel, *The Case for a Creator* (Grand Rapids, MI: Zondervan, 2004), 283.

2. Ibid., 283.

3. Ibid., 130.

4. Ibid., 287.

5. Genesis 1:1–3 (NIV).

6. Lee Strobel, *The Case for a Creator*, 78–91.

7. Ibid., 280.

8. Walter Isaacson, *Steve Jobs* (New York: Simon & Schuster, 2011), xxi.

9. Walter Isaacson, interview, *Fox & Friends*, October 31, 2011.

10. Mona Simpson, "A Sister's Eulogy for Steve Jobs," *New York Times*, October 30, 2011, www.nytimes.com/2011/10/30/opinion/mona-simpsons-eulogy-for-steve-jobs.html, accessed January 4, 2012.

AUTHOR Q&A

1. What prompted you to write *Divine Alignment*?
I have found that God, often through my readers, leads me to each new evolution of my journey as an author. Divine Alignment became the next evolution of the godwink thesis.

2. How would you describe what you mean by "Divine Alignment"?
Divine Alignment is the principle that we are all connected by invisible threads—godwink by godwink—on a grand GPS, God's Positioning System.

3. How is "mapping your destination" (as mentioned in chapter 3) different from spiritual consumerism?
"Mapping your destination" is aligned with the popular principle that we must establish goals for ourselves; as described by the *Alice in Wonderland* character in chapter 3, who said, "If you don't know where you're going, any road will take you there."

I find no relationship to "spiritual consumerism." I have always been fascinated with the manner in which different churches worship God, with varying forms of music and formats, and consider the concern that anyone would "shop around" to find a form that fits themselves, as probably non-relevant to God.

4. In the majority of the stories you share in the book, there is an element of healing, restoration, and celebration. Has there been a time in your life when you have experienced a "godwink" in the midst of a situation that didn't have a "happy ending"?
To me, an "unhappy godwink" would be like an "unhappy smile." There are situations where someone can experience a godwink in the midst of an unhappy situation, but inasmuch as a godwink is often another word for "answered prayer," we must consider each a blessing from God.

5. Have there been spiritual guides or mentors in your life who have helped you cultivate the kind of communication with God that you describe in chapter 1? If so, can you share what you learned from them?
My wonderful wife Louise is my most important spiritual guide. Her understanding of the scriptures is much, much deeper than mine. As well, I can say that such spiritual leaders as Dr. Norman Vincent Peale and Dr. Charles Stanley, both of whom I have been honored to know, were powerful mentors for me. Then there was a sweet, lesser known pastor, Ralph Lankler, who taught me to write a letter to God, every day, during a difficult time in my life; he too was a hero.

6. In chapter 2, "Listen to Your Inner Compass," you introduce readers to a woman who demonstrated incredible courage during World War II. She says, "One's first steps are always small" (p. 55). Can you share a time in your life when you took a small step toward listening to your inner compass?

The heroism of Irene Gut Opdyke in chapter 2 is so extraordinary that I could never imagine anything I have ever done as even being in the same ballpark.

As it relates to my own journey, taking the small steps of doing speaking engagements, wherever and whenever, just to get the experience and to develop my topics, led me to becoming an author. In talking about "so-called coincidences" in our lives—little experiences that happen to everyone, and which many of us have concluded could have come only from God—was a thesis that seemed to strike a chord with my listeners, which opened the pathway for my first book, *When God Winks*.

7. What was it like for you to write about your very personal story about the debt and shame that accompanied your "downsizing" from ABC? In these difficult economic times, what kind of advice or encouragement would you give to someone who has recently lost his or her job?
In sharing that story about a dark and desperate time in my life, I realized I was allowing God to shine the light on a sin—exposing my sin of pride. Prior to that writing, my pride caused me to "cover up" my being "fired" as a badge of dishonor.

The first step when you face anything catastrophic in your life, including the loss of a job, is to Talk to the Navigator, allowing God and your personal God's Positioning System to guide you in evaluating two important questions: What have I always *wanted* to do? How can I map my way there?

8. Have you ever experienced a "godwink" that prompted you to lay aside a personal dream or plan for the benefit of someone else?
I perhaps have. But, to tell you the truth, I am such an "obnoxious optimist" that I've always found the way to find the "positive" in any difficult situation.

One could build a case that the birth of my brain-injured son sty-mied my career growth at the ABC television network by limiting my time, focus, and freedom to travel for the company. On the other hand, that experience singularly brought me into a close walk with the Lord, kept me closer to home, and provided the opportunity to develop this series of books examining the thesis of how God speaks to us through godwinks.

9. Your biography on your website says that becoming an author and an inspirational speaker have always been "lifelong dreams." How do the principles you describe in *Divine Alignment* relate to the fulfillment of your dream?
The principles of Divine Alignment allow everyone to chart their own courses through life, arriving at a state of absolute contentment. It is only through the experiences in my own rearview mirror that I have the confirmation that these principles work. Simply put: When you step out in faith, heading for what you believe to be your des-tiny—or, as I've said to my son, "Your Job for God"—your pathways are certain to be lined with godwinks; people and events who are Divinely Aligned to be there, to help you get where you are going.

10. What is the main thing you hope people take away from read-ing *Divine Alignment*?
Hope. Hope is such a dear commodity in so many lives. People have faced so many hardships and tragedies that hope seems to be no-where in sight. But if through these simple principles—that God is speaking directly to you, out of seven billion people on this planet, every single day, through godwinks and people who are divinely aligned to help you along—if that can help you have just a little hope to get you going, I am doing my "Job for God."

11. You have been described as the "American Encourager." Where do you personally go to for encouragement?

I follow my own advice in chapter 1: I Talk to the Navigator. And if I'm not encouraged enough, I talk to my wonderful wife Louise. I sometimes suspect that she has God's personal phone number; when God doesn't answer me directly, I usually hear from Him through her.

12. *Divine Alignment* is a collection of powerful stories. Who is one of your favorite storytellers?

Dr. Norman Vincent Peale, author of *The Power of Positive Thinking*, was a model for me.